THE CALIFORNIA DIRECTORY OF
FINE WINERIES

SEVENTH EDITION

THE CALIFORNIA DIRECTORY OF
FINEWINERIES

K. REKA BADGER, CHERYL CRABTREE, DANIEL MANGIN,
AND MARTY OLMSTEAD, WRITERS

ROBERT HOLMES, PHOTOGRAPHER

TOM SILBERKLEIT, EDITOR AND PUBLISHER

WINE HOUSE PRESS

CONTENTS

INTRODUCTION

Whether you are a visitor or a native seeking the ultimate chalice of nectar from the grape, navigating Northern California's wine country can be intimidating. Hundreds of wineries —from glamorous estates to converted barns, from nationally recognized labels to hidden gems— are found throughout Napa, Sonoma, and Mendocino. The challenge is deciding where to go and how to plan a trip. This book will be your indispensable traveling companion.

The sixty-eight wineries in this fully updated, seventh edition of *The California Directory of Fine Wineries* are known for producing some of the world's most admired wines. From the moment you walk in the door of these wineries, you will be greeted like a guest and invited to sample at a relaxing, leisurely tempo. Although the quality of the winemaker's art is of paramount importance, the wineries are also notable as tourist destinations. Many boast award-winning contemporary architecture, while others are housed in lovingly preserved historical structures. Some have galleries featuring museum-quality art- work by local and international artists or exhibits focusing on the region's past and the history of wine- making. You will also enjoy taking informative behind-the-scenes tours, exploring inspirational gardens, and participating in celebrated culinary programs. With a bit of advance planning, you can arrange to take part in a barrel sampling, a blending seminar, or a grape stomping.

As you explore this magnificent region, you'll encounter some of California's most appealing scenery and attractions—mountain ranges, rugged coastline, pastures with majestic oak trees, abundant park- land, renowned spas, and historic towns. Use the information in this book to plan your trip, and be sure to stop along the way and take in the sights. You have my promise that traveling to your destination will be as pleasurable as the wine tasted upon your welcome.

—Tom Silberkleit
Editor and Publisher
Wine House Press
Sonoma, California

THE ETIQUETTE OF WINE TASTING

Most of the wineries profiled in this book offer amenities ranging from lush gardens to art exhibitions, but their main attraction is the tasting room. This is where winery employees get a chance to share their products and knowledge with consumers, in hopes of establishing a lifelong relationship. They are there to please.

Yet, for some visitors, the ritual of tasting fine wines can be intimidating. Perhaps it's because swirling wine and using a spit bucket seem to be unnatural acts. But with a few tips, even a first-time taster can enjoy the experience. After all, the point of tasting is to enhance your knowledge by learning the differences among varieties of wines, styles of winemaking, and appellations.

A list of available wines is usually posted, beginning with whites and ending with the heaviest reds or, if available, dessert wines. Look for the tasting notes, which are typically set out on the counter; refer to them as you taste each wine. A number of wineries charge a tasting fee for four or five wines of your choosing or for a "flight"—most often several preselected wines. In any event, the tasting process is the same.

After you are served, hold the stem of the glass with your thumb and as many fingers as you need to maintain control. Lift the glass up to the light and note the color and intensity of the wine. Good wines tend to be bright, with the color fading near the rim. Next, gently swirl the wine in the glass. Observe how much of the wine adheres to the sides of the glass. If lines—called legs—are visible, the wine is viscous, indicating body or weight as well as a high alcohol content. Now, tip the glass to about a 45-degree angle, take a short sniff, and concentrate on the aromas. Swirl the wine again to aerate it, releasing additional aromas. Take another sniff and see if the "bouquet" reminds you of anything—rose petals, citrus fruit, or a freshly ironed pillowcase, for example—that will help you identify the aroma.

Finally, take a sip and swirl the wine around your tongue, letting your taste buds pick up all the flavors. The wine may remind you of honey or cherries or mint—as with the "nosing," try to make as many associations as you can. Then spit the wine into the bucket on the counter. Afterward, notice how long the flavor stays in your mouth; a long finish is the ideal. If you don't want another taste, just pour the wine remaining in your glass into the bucket and move on. Remember, the more you spit or pour out, the more wines you will enjoy sampling.

The next level of wine tasting involves guided tastings and food-and-wine pairings. In these sessions, a few cheeses or a series of appetizers are paired with a flight of wines, usually a selection of three red or three white wines presented in the recommended order of tasting. The server will explain what goes with what.

If you still feel self-conscious, practice at home. Once you are in a real tasting room, you'll be better able to focus on the wine itself. That's the real payoff, because once you learn what you like and why you like it, you'll be able to recognize wines in a similar vein anywhere in the world.

WHAT IS AN APPELLATION?

Winemakers often showcase the source of their fruit by citing an *appellation* to describe the area where the grapes were grown. An appellation is a specific region that, in the United States, was traditionally determined by political borders such as state and county lines. Since the institution in 1981 of a system of American Viticultural Areas (AVAs), those borders have been based on climate and geography. Preexisting politically defined appellations were grandfathered into the new system of AVAs, administered these days by the U.S. Alcohol and Tobacco Tax and Trade Bureau (TTB). Using the name of either an appellation or an AVA on a label requires that a certain percentage of the wine in the bottle (75 and 85 percent, respectively) be made from grapes grown within the designation.

AVAs, in contrast to appellations, are defined by such natural features as soil types, prevailing winds, rivers, and mountain ranges. Wineries or other interested parties hoping to create an AVA must submit documented research to the TTB proving that the area's specific attributes distinguish it from the surrounding region. The TTB has the authority to approve or deny the petition.

Winemakers know that identifying the origin of their grapes can lend prestige to a wine, particularly if the AVA or appellation has earned a reputation for quality. It also provides information about what's inside the bottle. For instance, informed consumers know that a Chardonnay from the Napa Valley is apt to differ in both aroma and taste from a Sonoma Coast Chardonnay. When a winery uses grapes from an off-site AVA or appellation to make a particular wine, the label indicates the source of the fruit, not the location of the winery.

The following are the appellations in Napa, Sonoma, and Mendocino, which themselves are part of the larger North Coast appellation.

NAPA

Atlas Peak
Calistoga
Chiles Valley
Coombsville
Diamond Mountain District
Howell Mountain
Los Carneros
Mt. Veeder
Napa Valley
North Coast
Oak Knoll District of Napa Valley
Oakville
Rutherford
Spring Mountain District
St. Helena
Stags Leap District
Wild Horse Valley
Yountville

SONOMA

Alexander Valley
Bennett Valley
Chalk Hill
Dry Creek Valley
Fort Ross–Seaview
Green Valley of
    Russian River Valley
Knights Valley
Los Carneros
Moon Mountain District
    Sonoma County
North Coast
Northern Sonoma
Pine Mountain–Cloverdale Peak
Rockpile
Russian River Valley
Sonoma Coast
Sonoma Mountain
Sonoma Valley

MENDOCINO

Anderson Valley
Cole Ranch
Covelo
Dos Rios
McDowell Valley
Mendocino
Mendocino Ridge
North Coast
Pine Mountain–Cloverdale Peak
Potter Valley
Redwood Valley
Sanel Valley (pending)
Ukiah Valley (pending)
Yorkville Highlands

Napa

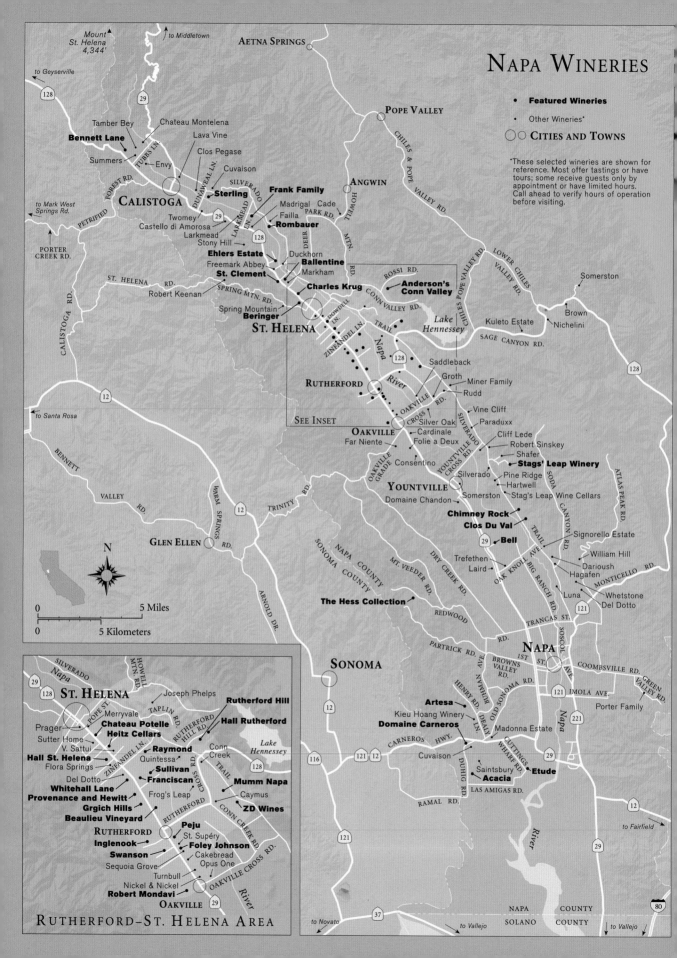

NAPA WINERIES

- ● **Featured Wineries**
- · Other Wineries*
- ◯◯ CITIES AND TOWNS

*These selected wineries are shown for reference. Most offer tastings or have tours; some receive guests only by appointment or have limited hours. Call ahead to verify hours of operation before visiting.

Mount St. Helena 4,344'

to Middletown

AETNA SPRINGS

to Geyserville

128

29

POPE VALLEY

CHILES & POPE VALLEY RD.

Tamber Bey
Chateau Montelena
Bennett Lane
Lava Vine
Summers
Clos Pegase
Envy

TUBBS LN.

FOREST RD.

PETRIFIED

DUNAWEAL LN.

SILVERADO

LARKMEAD LN.

to Mark West Springs Rd.

CALISTOGA

29

Sterling

Frank Family

Madrigal   Cade
Twomey   Failla
Castello di Amorosa **Rombauer**
Larkmead
Stony Hill

128

ANGWIN

HOWELL MTN. RD.

CADE PARK RD.

DEER

PORTER CREEK RD.

CALISTOGA RD.

ST. HELENA RD.

SPRING MTN. RD.

Ehlers Estate
Freemark Abbey   **Ballentine**
St. Clement   Markham
Robert Keenan
Spring Mountain
Beringer

Duckhorn

Charles Krug

Anderson's Conn Valley

ROSSI RD.

CONN VALLEY RD.

LOWER CHILES VALLEY RD.

Somerston

to Santa Rosa

12

ST. HELENA

POWELL LN.

ZINFANDEL LN.

NAPA TRAIL

Lake Hennessey

SAGE CANYON RD.

Brown
Nichelini

Kuleto Estate

128

RUTHERFORD

128

Napa River

OAKVILLE CROSS RD.

Saddleback
Groth
Miner Family
Rudd

SILVERADO TRAIL

128

BENNETT VALLEY RD.

WARM SPRINGS RD.

12

GLEN ELLEN

TRINITY RD.

OAKVILLE GRADE

OAKVILLE
Far Niente

Silver Oak
Cardinale
Folie a Deux
Consentino

YOUNTVILLE CROSS RD.

Vine Cliff
Paraduxx
Cliff Lede
Robert Sinskey
Shafer
Stags' Leap Winery
Pine Ridge
Hartwell
Stag's Leap Wine Cellars

ATLAS PEAK RD.

N

YOUNTVILLE
Domaine Chandon

Silverado
Somerston

SODA CANYON RD.

Signorello Estate

William Hill
Darioush
Hagafen

MONTICELLO RD.

Chimney Rock
Clos Du Val

29   **Bell**

Trefethen
Laird

OAK KNOLL AVE.

BIG RANCH RD.

Luna

Whetstone
Del Dotto

NAPA COUNTY
SONOMA COUNTY

MT. VEEDER RD.

DRY CREEK RD.

SILVERADO TRAIL

0 ____ 5 Miles

0 ____ 5 Kilometers

The Hess Collection

REDWOOD

PARTRICK RD.

BUHMAN AVE.

HENRY RD.

DEALY LN.

OLD SONOMA RD.

BROWNS VALLEY RD.

TRANCAS ST.

1ST ST.

SOSCOL AVE.

COOMBSVILLE RD.

GREEN VALLEY RD.

NAPA

121

IMOLA AVE.

221

Porter Family

to Fairfield

12

SONOMA

12

121

116

121

12

Artesa
Kieu Hoang Winery
Domaine Carneros

CARNEROS HWY.

Cuvaison

Madonna Estate

CUTTINGS WHARF RD.

DUHIG RD.

29

121

Etude

Saintsbury
Acacia

LAS AMIGAS RD.

RAMAL RD.

Napa River

29

37

to Novato

to Vallejo

NAPA   COUNTY
SOLANO COUNTY

to Vallejo

80

RUTHERFORD–ST. HELENA AREA

SILVERADO

HOWELL MTN. RD.

Napa

29

128

St. Helena

Joseph Phelps

TAPLIN RD.

Rutherford Hill

Merryvale
Chateau Potelle
Prager   **Heitz Cellars**
Sutter Home
V. Sattui   **Raymond**
Hall St. Helena
Flora Springs   Quintessa
Del Dotto   **Sullivan**
Whitehall Lane   **Franciscan**
Provenance and Hewitt
Grgich Hills   Frog's Leap
Beaulieu Vineyard

Hall Rutherford

RUTHERFORD HILL RD.

Conn Creek

Lake Hennessey

128

Mumm Napa
Caymus
ZD Wines

ZINFANDEL LN.

CONN CREEK RD.

RUTHERFORD RD.

TRAIL

Peju
Rutherford   St. Supéry
Inglenook   **Foley Johnson**
Swanson   Cakebread
Sequoia Grove   Opus One
Turnbull
Nickel & Nickel
Robert Mondavi

OAKVILLE

OAKVILLE CROSS RD.

River

29

The Napa Valley, jam-packed with hundreds of premium wineries and thousands of acres of coveted vineyards, has earned its position as the country's number one winemaking region. From its southern tip at San Pablo Bay, about an hour's drive from San Francisco, this picture-perfect patchwork of agriculture extends thirty miles north to the dramatic Palisades that tower above Calistoga. The narrow, scenic valley is defined on the east by a series of hills known as the Vaca Range and on the west by the rugged peaks of the Mayacamas Range, including the steep for- ested slopes of Mount Veeder. St. Helena, where upscale stores and chic boutiques line the historic Main Street, is the jewel in the region's crown. At the southern end of the valley, the city of Napa has experienced a boom in recent years, with a plethora of restaurants and attractions such as the vibrant Oxbow Public Market. The mostly two-lane Highway 29 links these and smaller towns that welcome visitors with a variety of spas, restaurants, and bed-and-breakfast inns.

For an unforgettable impression, book a hot-air balloon ride or simply drive up the winding Oakville Grade and pull over at the top for a view worthy of a magazine cover.

ACACIA VINEYARD

Acacia Vineyard ranks among the Pinot Noir pioneers of the Carneros appellation, a region of farmland and tidal marshes stretching north from San Pablo Bay. Due to the proximity of the bay, the winery basks in a maritime climate of morning fog and ocean breezes. Air temperatures average ten degrees cooler than those in upper Napa Valley, making Carneros perfect for growing the winery's specialties: Pinot Noir and Chardonnay.

Founded in 1979, the winery initially bought fruit from St. Clair Vineyard, a neighbor across the street. With its inaugural harvest, Acacia Vineyard became one of the first in California to produce a single-vineyard Pinot Noir. The winery continues to craft Pinot Noir from the old Martini clones growing in the dry-farmed St. Clair Vineyard, a vinicultural legacy that represents one of the nation's longest runs of consecutive bottlings of wine purchased from a single vineyard. Lone Tree Vineyard—named for an ancient acacia growing among the vines—is an estate planting that boasts thirteen different Pinot Noir clones. The winery's Chardonnay comes from both estate and purchased fruit grown in Carneros, with several single-vineyard offerings sourced from the Russian River Valley appellation.

An important stop along the Pacific Flyway, the Carneros region hosts many birds, including more than two dozen species of waterfowl, as well as egrets, western bluebirds, and red-tailed hawks. It is also home to threatened or endangered species. To help support them, Acacia makes a special wine, Marsh Chardonnay, sold exclusively at the winery, and donates proceeds from sales of the wine to a fund dedicated to the restoration and ongoing care of local wetlands.

An elongated complex of cocoa-brown buildings, Acacia Vineyard is a working winery with the crush pad located in front. Tucked beside the cellar, the boutique-style tasting room features a rustic chandelier and furnishings that convey a farm-to-table feeling. Glass doors open into one of the massive white barrel rooms containing hundreds of American and French and other European oak barrels.

On weekends, tastings frequently take place in the cellar, among stainless steel tanks emitting the fruity aroma of wine in various stages of development. As visitors gather around the long wood tasting bar, the scene evokes the intimate wine country experience of thirty years ago. On clear days, visitors stepping out the front door of the tasting room can see San Pablo Bay glittering in the distance, as well as 2,571-foot Mount Tamalpais to the southwest, 3,848-foot Mount Diablo to the southeast, and buildings rising from the heart of San Francisco fifty miles away.

ACACIA VINEYARD
2750 Las Amigas Rd.
Napa, CA 94559
707-226-9991, ext. 2
877-226-1700, ext. 2
acacia.info@acacia
vineyard.com
acaciavineyard.com

OWNER: Diageo Chateau and Estate Wines.

LOCATION: About 5 miles southwest of the town of Napa.

APPELLATION: Los Carneros.

HOURS: 10 A.M.–4 P.M. Monday–Saturday; noon–4 P.M. Sunday.

TASTINGS: $20–$25 for 5 or 6 wines. Reservations required.

TOURS: 11 A.M. Monday–Saturday.

THE WINES: Chardonnay, Pinot Noir, Syrah, Viognier.

SPECIALTIES: Single-vineyard Chardonnay and Pinot Noir.

WINEMAKER: Matthew Glynn.

ANNUAL PRODUCTION: 90,000 cases.

OF SPECIAL NOTE: Most single-vineyard wines available only in tasting room.

NEARBY ATTRACTION: di Rosa (indoor and outdoor exhibits of works by contemporary Bay Area artists).

ANDERSON'S CONN VALLEY VINEYARDS

ANDERSON'S CONN VALLEY VINEYARDS
680 Rossi Rd.
St. Helena, CA 94574
707-963-8600
800-946-3497
info@connvalleyvineyards
.com
connvalleyvineyards.com

OWNERS: Anderson family.

LOCATION: 3.3 miles east of Silverado Trail via Howell Mountain Rd. and Conn Valley Rd.

APPELLATION: Napa Valley.

HOURS: 9 A.M.–5 P.M. Monday–Friday; 10 A.M.–2 P.M. Saturday–Sunday.

TASTINGS: By appointment.

TOURS: By appointment.

THE WINES: Cabernet Franc, Cabernet Sauvignon, Chardonnay, Merlot, Pinot Noir, Sauvignon Blanc.

SPECIALTIES: Cabernet Sauvignon, Bordeaux blends.

WINEMAKERS: Todd Anderson and Robert Hunt.

ANNUAL PRODUCTION: 6,500 cases.

OF SPECIAL NOTE: Reserve cave tasting ($65) and private tasting with food pairing hosted by winemaker ($250).

NEARBY ATTRACTIONS: Bothe-Napa State Park (hiking, picnicking, horseback riding, swimming Memorial Day–Labor Day); Robert Louis Stevenson Museum (author memorabilia).

Less than a ten-minute drive from bustling downtown St. Helena, Anderson's Conn Valley Vineyards occupies a niche in a valley within a valley. The location is so remote that most drivers along Conn Valley Road aren't even aware the winery exists. Out here, you could hear a pin drop, except during the busy harvest season that begins in late summer.

Anderson's Conn Valley Vineyards was founded in 1983 by Todd Anderson and his parents, Gus and Phyllis. Gus Anderson spearheaded the lengthy search for vineyard property in Napa Valley. He had the advantage of realizing Napa's tremendous potential before the region became widely known (in the wake of the famous 1976 Paris tasting that put Napa on the world wine map) and before land in wine country became prohibitively expensive.

Joseph Heitz and Joseph lished wineries in the neighAndersonsAndersons found their dream ern part of the St. Helena near the base of Howell the acreage was not for sale; of negotiations to secure  Phelps had already established wineries in the neighborhood by the time the site, forty acres in the eastAmerican Viticultural Area Mountain. Unfortunately, it would take fifteen months the property.

Then the real work of establishing a winery operation began, and for the most part, it has all been done by the Andersons. Todd Anderson left his profession as a geophysicist to pound posts, hammer nails, and install twenty-six and a half acres of prime vineyards. That was just the beginning. While the vines matured, the Andersons created a fifteen-acre-foot reservoir and built the winery, the residence, and a modest cave system.

The family did hire professionals with the necessary heavy-duty equipment to expand the caves by 8,000 square feet. Completed in 2001, the 9,000-square-foot caves feature a warren of narrow pathways beneath the hillside. Deep in the caverns, one wall has been pushed out to make way for tables and chairs where visitors can sample the wines. In clement weather, tastings are often held on the far side of the caves, with seating beneath market umbrellas at an inviting arrangement of tables that overlook the reservoir.

The highly educational tastings are conducted by one of the knowledgeable Anderson's Conn staff members and frequently by owner Todd Anderson. A great advantage to touring a family winery is the chance to get to know the people behind the wines and to linger long enough to ask questions that might never get answered during a large group tour at one of Napa's big and better-known wineries located along either Highway 29 or the Silverado Trail.

ARTESA VINEYARDS & WINERY

In 1988 Codorníu Raventós, a Spanish producer known for Cava sparkling wines, commissioned the Barcelona-based architect Domingo Triay to design a hilltop winery on its 350-acre Napa Valley Carneros estate. The winery is submerged discreetly into the hillside behind three bermlike terraces, and its broad entry plaza is reached via a grand three-tiered concrete staircase edged by slender waterfalls.

Jackrabbits, quail, and other creatures often dart across Artesa's driveway as it gently switchbacks past open grassland and rows of Pinot Noir and Chardonnay, to the parking area. Here, atop the lowest terrace, a circular fountain edged by six spikelike, seven-foot-tall aluminum-composite sculptures by Artesa's artist in of Napa, hints at the splendor of the staircase, a long, another fountain — metal and set at dramatic forty-way to a grassy expanse. way is the winery, its mostly

residence, Gordon Huether to come. At the top landing narrow oval pool with columns spaced wide apart five-degree angles — gives Farther west along the walk-grass-covered exterior punc-tuated by the tasting room's entrance and panels of tinted glass that form an inverted pyramid.

First-time visitors often find themselves so awestruck by the architecture and the south-facing views — on clear days extending south past the di Rosa art preserve and San Pablo Bay all the way to San Francisco — that a few minutes pass before their eyes drift east and north to equally captivating views of vineyards, grazing land, and the Vaca Range. Inside the winery, a concierge escorts guests to tastings at one of several bars or tables in the gallerylike indoor space, at an open-air interior courtyard, or on an outdoor terrace facing south. All the spaces invite lingering over a lineup of fine wines built around Napa Valley Chardonnays and Pinot Noirs that also includes Cabernet Sauvignons and two wines from Spanish varietals: Albariño and Tempranillo, a stylishly earthy red.

Artesa means "handcrafted" in Catalan, and the hands crafting Artesa's wines belong to Mark Beringer, a great-great-grandson of Jacob Beringer, a nineteenth-century Napa Valley winemaking pioneer. Under Beringer, the Artesa style emphasizes holding true to a varietal's characteristics and expressing the geology and climate of the vineyards where the grapes are grown. Artesa Pinot Noirs taste like classic Pinots, and among the pleasures of a tasting here is experiencing the flavor variations depending on the vineyards the grapes come from. Reflecting Artesa's commitment to responsible land management, those vineyards are farmed using certified sustainable practices.

ARTESA VINEYARDS & WINERY
1345 Henry Rd.
Napa, CA 94559
707-224-1668
info@artesawinery.com
artesawinery.com

OWNERS: Codorníu Raventós family.

LOCATION: 6 miles southwest of downtown Napa, off Old Sonoma Rd.

APPELLATIONS: Los Carneros, Napa Valley.

HOURS: 10 A.M.–5 P.M. daily (last full tasting at 4:30 P.M.).

TASTINGS: $20 for 4 wines; $25 for 5 reserve and limited-release wines. Food-and-wine pairings daily (reservations required).

TOURS: 11 A.M. and 2 P.M. daily.

THE WINES: Albariño, Cabernet Franc, Cabernet Sauvignon, Chardonnay, Merlot, Pinot Noir, Rosé of Pinot Noir, Sauvignon Blanc, Tempranillo.

SPECIALTIES: Codorníu Napa Grand Reserve sparkling wine, estate-grown Chardonnay and Pinot Noir.

WINEMAKER: Mark Beringer.

ANNUAL PRODUCTION: 50,000 cases.

OF SPECIAL NOTE: Codorníu Raventós family's winemaking history in Spain dates back to 1551. Underground aging cellar cooled naturally by surrounding earth. Many works by artist-in-residence Gordon Huether on exhibit. Cheese and charcuterie plates available. Many reserve and limited-release wines available only in tasting room.

NEARBY ATTRACTION: di Rosa (indoor and outdoor exhibits of works by contemporary Bay Area artists).

BALLENTINE VINEYARDS

BALLENTINE VINEYARDS
2820 St. Helena Hwy.
North
St. Helena, CA 94574
707-963-7919
info@ballentinevineyards
.com
ballentinevineyards.com

OWNERS: Van and Betty
Ballentine.

LOCATION: 3 miles north
of St. Helena on east side
of St. Helena Hwy.

APPELLATIONS: St. Helena,
Napa Valley.

HOURS: 10 A.M.–5 P.M. daily.

TASTINGS: $10. Reservations
required.

TOURS: By appointment.

THE WINES: Cabernet Franc,
Cabernet Sauvignon,
Chardonnay, Chenin
Blanc, Malvasia Bianca,
Merlot, Petit Verdot, Petite
Sirah, Syrah, Zinfandel.

SPECIALTIES: Cabernet
Franc, Chardonnay,
Malvasia Bianca Frizzante,
Petit Verdot, Petite Sirah.

WINEMAKER: Bruce Devlin.

ANNUAL PRODUCTION:
10,000 cases.

OF SPECIAL NOTE: Reserve
Chardonnay and Reserve
Cabernet Sauvignon sold
only in tasting room.
Zinfandel Port-style wine
available.

NEARBY ATTRACTIONS:
Bothe-Napa State Park
(hiking, picnicking,
horseback riding,
swimming Memorial Day–
Labor Day); Bale Grist
Mill State Historic park
(water-powered mill circa
1846); Culinary Institute
of America at Greystone
(cooking demonstrations);
Robert Louis Stevenson
Museum (author
memorabilia).

Longtime locals Betty and Van Ballentine grew up in the wine business. In fact, their combined family histories represent more than a century of Napa Valley winemaking. The couple met as teenagers and married more than sixty years ago. Since then, they have continued to grow grapes and make wine just as their parents and grandparents did, offering visitors classic varieties and old-world hospitality.

Born in Italy, Betty's grandfather immigrated to California in 1884 and helped plant the vineyards at what would become Korbel Champagne Cellars. In 1906 he moved to Calistoga, planted

his own sixty-acre vineyard, and built a winery. After Betty's grandfather died, her father and uncle operated the winery until closing its doors in 1963. The old vineyard near Calistoga lives on under the care of the Ballentines and supplies extraordinary fruit for several wines, including the reserve Zinfandel. The Ballentines recently planted new Cabernet Sauvignon and Malbec vines on a portion of the vineyard.

Van, an experienced viticulturist, spent his formative years working in the St. Helena–area vineyard and winery his father purchased in 1922. The elder Ballentine dubbed his brand Deer Park, after the family farm in Ireland. In 1944 Van and his father acquired twenty-five acres just north of St. Helena. Currently planted to Merlot, Syrah, and Malvasia Bianca, the land is called Betty's Vineyard. It is home to Ballentine Vineyards, as well as to Betty and Van, who live in a hundred-year-old farmhouse on the property.

After his father's winery closed in 1959, Van continued to farm wine grapes. He spent a half-dozen years managing the vineyards at Christian Brothers Winery. But he yearned to return to winemaking, so in 1992 he and Betty revived the Deer Park winery and launched Ballentine Vineyards. Three years later, they built a solar-powered winery with an attached tasting room opposite Betty's Vineyard. Remodeled in 2009, the intimate tasting room blooms with tropical greenery, and friendly staff members offer a warm greeting. Espresso-stained cabinetry and black granite countertops complement the blue-gray flagstone flooring and cut crystal counter buckets.

The Ballentines source their fruit from three estate vineyards, including the sixteen-acre Crystal Springs Vineyard, near Howell Mountain. They purchased the land in 1949 and planted Petite Sirah and Petit Verdot. Syrah planted in 1960 at Crystal Springs Vineyard remains the oldest Syrah in Napa Valley. In 2002 the Ballentines named Bruce Devlin as their winemaker. Van continues to tend the vineyards, and both Van and Betty keep a close eye on wines bottled under the family name.

BEAULIEU VINEYARD

French immigrant and winemaker Georges de Latour and his wife, Fernande, bought their first Rutherford ranch in 1900. "Beau lieu!" Fernande declared when she saw the ranch, deeming it a "beautiful place." Thus, Beaulieu Vineyard, also known simply as BV, was named. Among the first to recognize Rutherford's potential for yielding stellar Cabernet Sauvignon, Georges de Latour was determined to craft wine to rival the French. By 1909 he had expanded his vineyard and established a nursery for cultivating phylloxera-resistant rootstock. For a time, the nursery supplied a half-million grafted vines annually to California vineyards.

In 1938 de Latour hired fabled, Russian-born enologist André Tchelistcheff, who declared the 1936 Private Reserve Cabernet Sauvignon worthy of flagship status. With de Latour's blessing, he introduced a number of practices now considered standard, including controlling heat during fermentation to keep wines cool and protect delicate fruit flavors, and barrel aging in French, rather than American, oak barrels for the addition of more nuanced components. As a result, BV's Private Reserve became Napa Valley's first "cult Cab" and continues to rank among the region's most widely collected wines.

Housed in a Boston ivy–clad complex built in three different centuries, the gray stone and concrete winery faces the visitor center across a parking lot studded with sycamores and oaks. Guests follow a path edged with manicured boxwood and roses to reach the center, a two-story, hexagonal building with stone exterior. Upon entering, they are immediately handed a complimentary glass of wine in homage to Mrs. de Latour's peerless hospitality. Natural light spills from above, bathing the redwood interior. A curved staircase leads down an open well to the Club Room, where visitors who reserve ahead can enjoy a seated tasting.

A few steps from the visitor center is the Reserve Room, dedicated to the winery's flagship Georges de Latour Private Reserve Cabernet Sauvignon. At a softly lit marble-topped bar, visitors can taste winery exclusives and library wines, or purchase vintages of the Private Reserve going back to 1970. Fieldstone walls mimic those of BV's core winery, built in 1885. In a cozy side room, a glass-topped table displays bottles representing singular moments in the winery's history, including a release of Pure Altar Wine vinified during Prohibition. A brilliant businessman, de Latour prospered despite grape shortages, insect infestations, and Prohibition. More than a century later, Beaulieu Vineyard reigns as a leader in the production of acclaimed Cabernet Sauvignon and is among the longest continually operating wineries in Napa Valley.

BEAULIEU VINEYARD
1960 St. Helena Hwy.
Rutherford, CA 94573
800-264-6918, ext. 5233
707-967-5233
visitingbv@bvwines.com
bvwines.com

OWNER: Diageo Chateau and Estate Wines.

LOCATION: About 3 miles south of St. Helena.

APPELLATION: Rutherford.

HOURS: 10 A.M.–5 P.M. daily.

TASTINGS: Maestro Wine Tasting, $20 for choice of 4 wines from winery-only Maestro series. Reserve Tasting, $35 for current and library Georges de Latour Private Reserve Cabernet Sauvignon. Retrospective Reserve Tasting, $50 for a flight of 4 Georges de Latour Private Reserve Cabernet Sauvignon.

TOURS: Historic Tour and Barrel Tasting ($20) includes tour of the 1885 winery and BV museum; reservations required.

THE WINES: Cabernet Sauvignon, Chardonnay, Merlot, Sauvignon Blanc.

SPECIALTIES: Rutherford Cabernet Sauvignon, Georges de Latour Private Reserve Cabernet Sauvignon.

WINEMAKER: Jeffrey Stambor.

ANNUAL PRODUCTION: Unavailable.

OF SPECIAL NOTE: 15 small-lot wines available only in tasting room. Clone series (Cabernet Sauvignon) and Reserve Tapestry series (Bordeaux blends) available in the Reserve Room.

NEARBY ATTRACTION: Culinary Institute of America at Greystone (cooking demonstrations).

BELL WINE CELLARS

BELL WINE CELLARS
6200 Washington St.
Yountville, CA 94599
707-944-1673
info@bellwine.com
bellwine.com

OWNERS: Anthony A. Bell in partnership with the Spanos and Berberian families.

LOCATION: 1 mile south of downtown Yountville.

APPELLATIONS: Yountville, St. Helena, Calistoga, Mt. Veeder, Rutherford, Napa Valley, Sierra Foothills.

HOURS: 10 A.M.–4 P.M. (time of last tasting) daily, by appointment.

TASTINGS: $20 for 4 or 5 current-release wines; $40 for 4 or 5 reserve wines. By appointment.

TOURS: On the hour 10 A.M.–4 P.M., by appointment.

THE WINES: Cabernet Sauvignon, Chardonnay, Merlot, Sauvignon Blanc, Syrah.

SPECIALTY: Single-clone Cabernet Sauvignon, especially Clone 6.

WINEMAKER: Anthony A. Bell.

ANNUAL PRODUCTION: 12,000–14,000 cases.

OF SPECIAL NOTE: Patio tasting area with views of estate Chardonnay and Merlot grapes and beyond them the Mayacamas Mountains. Most wines available only in tasting room.

NEARBY ATTRACTION: Napa Valley Museum (winemaking displays, art exhibits).

Situated only a mile south of downtown Yountville but at the end of a long, quiet access road that makes it feel off the beaten path, Bell Wine Cellars was founded by Anthony Bell, known for his Old World–style Cabernet Sauvignons and research into Cabernet clones. Bell grew up on a wine estate in his native South Africa owned by his father's employer, a major spirits and wine distributor, and by his late teens had become passionate about winemaking. To further his son's wine education, Bell's father arranged for him to work first at a winery that the distributor owned in Spain's sherry district and later at Château Loudenne, a major Bordeaux producer.

After graduating with a master's degree in enology from the University of California, Davis, Bell landed a job in 1979 as assistant  winemaker and viticulturist at Napa Valley's Beaulieu Vineyard. While at Beaulieu, Bell brought together grape growers and wine- makers, a novel idea at the time, to discuss ways to elevate wine quality. Bell also drew the bound- aries for the Carneros appellation and was involved in establishing the Oakville and Rutherford appellations. Bell's duties as Beaulieu's viticulturist led to his participation in a fascinating experiment tracking fourteen types of Cabernet Sauvignon clones to see which produced the best wines. Each year for nearly a decade, grapes were grown and wines were made and tasted blindly. The wine that most often scored the highest was from Clone 6, a Cabernet type long in disuse that a U.C. Davis researcher had traced to an abandoned vineyard in California's Gold Country.

Bell left Beaulieu in the early 1990s to form the partnership that evolved into the current winery. Not surprisingly, his Clone 6 Rutherford Cabernet Sauvignon is the flagship offering. Two other Cabernets are made, but several other varietals are also represented, including Chardonnay and Merlot produced from estate-grown grapes. Bell credits his experiences in Europe, particularly Bordeaux, with influencing the restrained winemaking style for all his wines, which favor elegance and balance over bravado.

Though Bell has impressive winemaking credentials, a visit to his winery is a casual affair. Current-release tastings take place amid stainless steel tanks holding Sauvignon Blanc and other white wines and, if things get crowded, near oak barrels filled with Cabernet and other reds. Grape to Glass Tours begin where Bell first learned his craft—in the vineyards—for a brief discussion of how grapes grow. After visits to the tanks and barrels, tours conclude with wine-and-cheese pair- ings. For those intrigued by Bell's clonal investigations, there's a premium Cabernet-only tasting.

BENNETT LANE WINERY

Far from the din and traffic of central Napa Valley, Bennett Lane Winery lures adventuresome Cabernet Sauvignon lovers to the northernmost wedge of the valley, where the Vaca Range meets the Mayacamas Range. This sequestered setting just north of the town of Calistoga features dramatic views of Mount St. Helena and the Palisades, which provide an ideal backdrop for Bennett Lane's handcrafted, small-lot wines. Bennett Lane's signature wine is named Maximus, after the second-century Roman emperor Magnus Maximus, a noted vinophile of his day. The exact percentages of varietals that go into the Maximus wines vary somewhat from vintage to vintage. The Maximus Red Feasting Wine is a unique blend, made primarily from Cabernet

Sauvignon, with the addition of 20 percent or so Merlot, as well as a small amount of Syrah and, sometimes, Petit Verdot. At Bennett Lane, blending is the name of the game, and tasters eager to learn more about this elusive art are invited to take part in a special program whereby they taste and combine a selection of varietals to create their own Maximus blend.

Visitors to the Mediterranean-style winery are welcomed into a tasting room painted in warm tones of brown and Tuscan gold. Enhancements added during a 2012 remodel include upholstered armchairs for relaxing and a Brazilian granite tasting bar. In order to provide a tasting experience that is enjoyable and educational, as well as interactive, iPads have been mounted along the bar. Here visitors can access a dynamic application that describes Bennett Lane wines and their source vineyards. The app also delivers the latest reviews, detailed tasting notes, and tempting recipes to pair with the wines. The iPads make it easy for tasters to share their wine discoveries with friends via social media, or enter and e-mail their tasting notes to fellow wine lovers.

Owners Randy and Lisa Lynch were relative newcomers to the world of wine in 2003, when they purchased what had once been a custom crush facility. Originally, they had been looking for a second home with vineyard land, and soon after purchasing a residence in Calistoga, they bought the Bennett Lane property. The Lynches were encouraged by critical praise for their wines, whose fruit now comes from highly acclaimed sources in Napa Valley. These vineyards are dotted throughout the valley, from Yountville in the south to Randy Lynch's vineyard in Calistoga in the north. Lynch's goal is to create wines that are both approachable and complex, what he calls "the best of both worlds, meaning you can drink them today, but they are structured enough to cellar for several years."

BENNETT LANE WINERY
3340 Hwy. 128
Calistoga, CA 94515
877-629-6272
info@bennettlane.com
bennettlane.com

OWNERS: Randy and Lisa Lynch.

LOCATION: About 2 miles north of Calistoga.

APPELLATION: Napa Valley.

HOURS: 10 A.M.–5:30 P.M. daily.

TASTINGS: $15 for 4 wines; $40 for Reserve Cabernet Sauvignon.

TOURS: Daily, by appointment.

THE WINES: Cabernet Sauvignon, Chardonnay, Maximus (red blend), White Maximus (white blend).

SPECIALTIES: Cabernet Sauvignon, Maximus.

WINEMAKER: Rob Hunter.

ANNUAL PRODUCTION: 12,000 cases.

OF SPECIAL NOTE: Varietals Fruit Flavor Custom Blend Experience, by appointment ($225 per person) and including a tour and tasting of current releases with cheese pairing, allows visitors to create and bottle their own wine. Annual events include Cabernet Release Weekend (February). Reserve Chardonnay and Syrah available only in tasting room.

NEARBY ATTRACTIONS: Old Faithful Geyser of California; Robert Louis Stevenson State Park (hiking).

BERINGER VINEYARDS

BERINGER VINEYARDS
2000 Main St.
St. Helena, CA 94574
866-708-9463
beringer.com

LOCATION: On Hwy. 29 about .5 mile north of St. Helena.

APPELLATION: Napa Valley.

HOURS: 10 A.M.–5 P.M. daily in winter; until 6 P.M. in summer.

TASTINGS AND TOURS: Various options are available. Check beringer.com for information and reservations.

THE WINES: Cabernet Sauvignon, Chardonnay, Merlot, red blends.

SPECIALTIES: Private Reserve Cabernet Sauvignon, single-vineyard Cabernet Sauvignon, Private Reserve Chardonnay.

WINEMAKER: Laurie Hook.

ANNUAL PRODUCTION: Unavailable.

OF SPECIAL NOTE: Tours include visit to barrel storage caves hand-chiseled in late 1800s.

NEARBY ATTRACTIONS: Bothe-Napa State Park (hiking, picnicking, horseback riding, swimming Memorial Day–Labor Day); Robert Louis Stevenson Museum (author memorabilia).

With its 1883 Rhine House and hand-carved aging tunnels, Beringer Vineyards is steeped in history like few other California wineries. Established in 1876, at the dawn of California wine, it is the only winery from that founding era that has never missed a vintage. Today, Beringer is widely recognized for combining established traditions with modern elegance.

It was German know-how and the vision that the Napa Valley could produce wines as fine as those from Europe that set the Beringer brothers on the path to glory. Jacob and Frederick Beringer emigrated from Mainz, Germany, to the United States in the 1860s. Jacob, having worked in cellars in Germany, was intrigued when he heard that the California climate was ideal for growing the varietal grapes that flourished in Europe's winemaking regions. Leaving Frederick in New York, he traveled west in 1870 to discover that Napa Valley's rocky, well-drained soils were similar to those in his native Rhine Valley. Five years later, he bought land with Frederick and began excavating the hillsides to create tunnels for aging his wines. During the building of the caves and winery, Jacob lived in an 1848 farmhouse that today is known as the Hudson House. The meticulously restored and expanded structure now serves as Beringer Vineyards' Culinary Arts Center.

The star attraction on the lavishly landscaped grounds is unquestionably the seventeen-room Rhine House, which Frederick modeled after his ancestral home in Germany. The redwood, brick, and stucco mansion is painted in the original Tudor color scheme of earth tones, and slate covers the gabled roof and exterior. The interior of the Rhine House is graced with extraordinary gems of craftsmanship, such as Belgian art nouveau–style stained-glass windows.

Beringer Vineyards was the first winery in Napa Valley to give public tours and continues the tradition today by offering two tours, each covering the winery and its fascinating history. An introductory tour takes visitors to the cellars and hand-dug aging tunnels in the Old Stone Winery, where they can also enjoy wine tasting. A longer, more in-depth tour, the Taste of Beringer, includes the demonstration vineyard, where visitors will learn about grape growing, and a wine tasting in the Rhine House, where they will hear about Beringer's winemaking techniques and experience firsthand how to taste wine like a professional.

CHARLES KRUG WINERY

A 2013 renovation of its colossal Redwood Cellar Building breathed splendid new life into Charles Krug, the Napa Valley's oldest operating winery. The cupola-topped structure, completed in 1874 and an official California Historic Landmark, is named for the 173 redwood aging and fermenting tanks—some as tall as nineteen feet and holding up to 36,000 gallons—that stored Krug wine into the 1990s.

Shots in the 1995 Keanu Reeves romance *A Walk in the Clouds,* set in post–World War II Napa Valley, depict the building jam-packed with aging tanks. In transforming the ground floor and mezzanine into a new hospitality center with a café and a tasting room, architect Howard Backen added a rustic, occasionally wine-soaked patina to his contemporary barn-chic design by repurposing the tanks' staves for the walls and ceilings. Other noteworthy touches by Backen include the stalwart twenty-seven-foot slab of stained and polished Douglas fir that serves as the tasting bar; the casually arranged settees, chairs, and stools for seated tastings; and the rows and rows of bottles labeled "1861" to commemorate the winery's birth year.

The sense of history fully cherished is palpable from the moment one enters the Redwood Cellar, all the more profoundly so on the mezzanine, where the cider press Charles Krug used in 1858 to make the Napa Valley's first commercial wine is exhibited. The mezzanine is among the stops on enlightening tours, conducted daily, that also include barrel tastings and a walk on the property. Krug, an immigrant who fled Prussia to avoid persecution for his democratic political views, was respected by his Napa Valley peers for his pioneering farming techniques and enthusiastic promotion of the valley as a wine region.

In 1943 Italian immigrants Cesare Mondavi and his wife, Rosa, purchased Krug for $75,000 from its only other owner. Run these days by the family of Peter Mondavi Sr. (Cesare's son and Robert Mondavi's brother), the winery specializes in Cabernet Sauvignon and other Bordeaux-style wines. Tours conclude in the library, its focal point a temperature-controlled display of seven decades' of the flagship Vintage Selection Cabernet Sauvignon, including a bottle from 1944, the family's inaugural production year. Recent vintages of this Cabernet are always part of the winery's Family Reserve tasting and sometimes the Limited Release one. Unlike newer Napa Valley wineries, Krug has a decades-old permit allowing an on-site restaurant. In 2014 Richard Haake, a noted local chef, designed the menu for Cucina di Rosa, which serves panini, salads, light meals, and espresso drinks to enjoy inside or at oak-shaded picnic tables on the landscaped grounds.

CHARLES KRUG WINERY
2800 Main St.
St. Helena, CA 94574
707-967-2229
info@charleskrug.com
charleskrug.com

OWNERS: Peter Mondavi Sr. family.

LOCATION: 1 mile north of downtown St. Helena.

APPELLATIONS: St. Helena, Howell Mountain, Los Carneros, Yountville.

HOURS: 10:30 A.M.–5 P.M. daily.

TASTINGS: For flights of 5 wines—$20 for Classic, $40 for Family Reserve, $50 for Limited Release.

TOURS: 10:30 A.M. Friday–Sunday; 10: 30 A.M. and 12:30 P.M. Monday–Thursday. By appointment.

THE WINES: Cabernet Sauvignon, Chardonnay, Merlot, Pinot Noir, Sauvignon Blanc.

SPECIALTIES: Limited Release Howell Mountain Cabernet Sauvignon, X Clones Cabernet Sauvignon, Estate Sauvignon Blanc, Bordeaux-style blended wines.

WINEMAKER: Stacy Clark.

ANNUAL PRODUCTION: 80,000 cases.

OF SPECIAL NOTE: Oldest winery in Napa Valley. Recently restored 1874 winery building and hospitality center designed by noted architect Howard Backen. Culinary Institute of America "farm to table" student garden. On-site restaurant. Picnic tables (reservations recommended). Two limited-release Cabernet Sauvignons and one Sauvignon Blanc available only in tasting room.

NEARBY ATTRACTION: Culinary Institute of America at Greystone (cooking demonstrations).

CHATEAU POTELLE

CHATEAU POTELLE
1200 Dowdell Ln.
St. Helena, CA 94574
707-255-9440
info@chateaupotelle.com
chateaupotelle.com

OWNER: Jean-Noel Fourmeaux.

LOCATION: .75 mile south of St. Helena.

APPELLATIONS: Mt. Veeder, Napa Valley.

HOURS: 10 A.M.–5 P.M. daily, by appointment.

TASTINGS: $35 for 4 wines; $45 for 4 wines and chef-prepared bites.

TOURS: None.

THE WINES: Chardonnay, Cabernet Franc, Cabernet Sauvignon, Merlot, Petite Sirah, Sauvignon Blanc, Syrah, Zinfandel.

SPECIALTIES: Cabernet Sauvignon, Zinfandel, Illegitimate (red blend), Inevitable (white blend), Rosé of Cinsault and Syrah, Zinie (late-harvest Zinfandel).

WINEMAKERS: Jean-Noel Fourmeaux and Sal Galvan.

ANNUAL PRODUCTION: 4,800 cases.

OF SPECIAL NOTE: Seated tastings held both indoors and outdoors. Cuisine for food-and-wine pairings conceived by chef Ken Frank of La Toque, perennial recipient of one-star Michelin Guides rating. Many wines available only in tasting room.

NEARBY ATTRACTIONS: Culinary Institute of America at Greystone (cooking demonstrations); Bale Grist Mill State Historic Park (water-powered mill circa 1846); Robert Louis Stevenson Museum (author memorabilia).

The lighthearted environment at this tasting house and garden just south of St. Helena's downtown comes courtesy of its ebullient French owner, Jean-Noel Fourmeaux. The whimsy begins at the yellow front door, which is actually the back door and can't even be opened: there's only a wall behind it. Around back at the true entrance, off Dowdell Lane, the quirkiness continues. Festive thin-metal Mexican chandeliers spray-painted white hang inside a lofty Moroccan tasting tent that's framed on one side by crape myrtle trees. Inside the bright white cottage, a dozen and a half hot-air balloon replicas dangle by monofilament from a ceiling painted warm blue.

Despite the playful ambience, it would be a mistake to assume that style trumps substance here. This is a vibrant and well-conceived space to enjoy seated, hosted tastings  (there's no stand-up bar) of handcrafted wines either by themselves or with meticulously prepared morsels from La Toque, a top-rated restaurant in the city of Napa. During summer, buckwheat soba noodles with a ginger-hoisin sesame vinaigrette might accompany Inevitable, a white blend, and chilled corn velouté with chèvre might complement a Chardonnay. For the reds, Moroccan spice-rubbed lamb might play off a Syrah (and vice versa), a sliver of Niman Ranch rib-eye the refined Cabernet Sauvignon. Cheerful multicolored placemats list the foods and wines being served.

Many Chateau Potelle wines come from grapes grown on Mount Veeder. This southern Napa Valley appellation is known for rocky, volcanic soils and growing conditions that produce smaller but more concentrated grapes than those on the valley floor. The cooler mountain temperatures require harvesting three or four weeks later, allowing grapes to ripen at a slower pace, adding character and complexity. Fourmeaux is prone to wax sensually poetic about Mount Veeder's virtues and how winemaking choices such as slow fermenting using the grapes' natural yeasts result in more characterful wines. As with his delightful space, what comes across when experiencing them is a sense of the pleasure, self-assurance, and wisdom that went into their creation.

The name Chateau Potelle comes from the medieval castle in France that Fourmeaux's family has owned for nine centuries. As he recounts the story, he first came to the Napa Valley to "spy" for the French government after sales here surged in the wake of Napa wines' strong showing in the 1976 Judgment of Paris tastings. He saw a niche for "California wines with a French accent," ones that embrace the exuberant flavors produced by California's climate and terrain but that also manifest poise and restraint. It's a niche he's filled with élan for three-plus decades now.

CHIMNEY ROCK WINERY

A quarter mile past the elegant wrought iron gates of Chimney Rock Winery, the broad face of the winery gleams beyond converging rows of meticulously farmed Cabernet Sauvignon vines. Whitewashed walls, arched doorways, and soaring gables define and distinguish the eye-catching architecture. Marking the eastern border of the Stags Leap District, the oak-studded Vaca Range is a dramatic backdrop for the winery and harbors the volcanic formation that gave the winery its name.

In 1980 Sheldon "Hack" Wilson, after multiple business successes, turned his talents and resources to making great wines. He, along with his wife, Stella, bought a pristine 185-acre property just south of Yountville and promptly planted 74 acres of Cabernet Sauvignon. By 1990 the couple had completed the tasting room and adjacent winery in the Cape Dutch style of Stella's native South Africa. For the winery's facade, the Wilsons commissioned a decorative frieze that depicts Ganymede — cupbearer to the mythical gods of ancient Greece — which gives the building a timeless, old-world feel. An avid gardener and horticulturist, Stella designed and planted elaborate beds surrounding both their home and the winery. The abundant gardens continue to flourish today.

In 2000 the Wilsons partnered with the Terlato family, whose participation in the wine industry had spanned more than fifty years and eleven wine-producing countries. Under the care and guidance of Tony, Bill, and John Terlato, an additional 60 acres were planted to Cabernet Sauvignon, and a new state-of-the-art winery facility was built. After Hack Wilson's death, the Terlato family assumed full ownership of the winery, a gem that includes 119 acres of vineyards devoted almost entirely to the winery's signature Cabernet Sauvignon and other Bordeaux varietals. Over the past decade, the Terlato family has carried the winery and its legacy forward by continuing to produce handcrafted, small-production, single-vineyard wines.

From behind the stately wine bar, staffers warmly greet guests. Just outside the tasting room, a patio with tables and lounge furniture arranged under a wisteria-draped arbor makes a perfect setting to relax with a glass of wine. From this vantage point, visitors can admire Ganymede, the gardens, and, beyond the old winery, the Stags Leap Palisades. To the east is the V-shaped formation where an indigenous Wappo hunter once reported seeing a legendary stag make a diversionary leap to save its herd from flying arrows.

Chimney Rock
Cabernet Sauvignon
Stags Leap District
Napa Valley
PRODUCED & BOTTLED BY CHIMNEY ROCK WINERY
NAPA, CALIFORNIA · ALCOHOL 14.1% BY VOLUME

CHIMNEY ROCK WINERY
5350 Silverado Trail
Napa, CA 94558
800-257-2641
707-257-2641
info@chimneyrock.com
chimneyrock.com

OWNERS: Terlato family.

LOCATION: 3 miles south of Yountville.

APPELLATION: Stags Leap District.

HOURS: 10 A.M.–5 P.M. daily.

TASTINGS: $35 for tasting of 4 or 5 wines; private seated tastings by appointment.

TOURS: Estate tour and tasting, barrel tasting, and VIP vineyard tour offered daily by appointment.

THE WINES: Cabernet Franc, Cabernet Sauvignon, Merlot, Petit Verdot, Sauvignon Blanc, Sauvignon Gris.

SPECIALTIES: 100 percent estate-grown single-vineyard Stags Leap District Cabernet Sauvignons, Elevage (red Bordeaux blend), Elevage Blanc (white Bordeaux blend).

WINEMAKER: Elizabeth Vianna.

ANNUAL PRODUCTION: 30,000 cases.

OF SPECIAL NOTE: Rotating display of artworks. Annual Vineyard to Vintner event (April) by Stags Leap District winegrowers. Winery is pet friendly.

NEARBY ATTRACTION: Napa Valley Museum (winemaking displays, art exhibits).

CLOS DU VAL

CLOS DU VAL
5330 Silverado Trail
Napa, CA 94558
707-261-5200
800-993-9463
cdv@closduval.com
closduval.com

OWNER: John Goelet.

LOCATION: 5 miles north of the town of Napa.

APPELLATION: Stags Leap District.

HOURS: 10 A.M.–5 P.M. daily.

TASTINGS: $15 for current releases; $25 for reserve tasting.

TOURS: By appointment.

THE WINES: Cabernet Sauvignon, Chardonnay, Merlot, Pinot Noir, Sauvignon Blanc.

SPECIALTY: Cabernet Sauvignon.

WINEMAKER: Kristy Melton.

ANNUAL PRODUCTION: 60,000 cases.

OF SPECIAL NOTE: Cabanas for outdoor tastings. *Pétanque* court and picnic areas. Demonstration vineyard for self-guided walks. Winery and picnic grounds are pet friendly. Private tastings by appointment.

NEARBY ATTRACTION: Napa Valley Museum (winemaking displays, art exhibits).

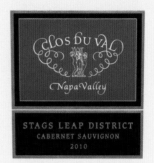

That this winery has a French name is not an affectation. Owner and cofounder John Goelet's mother was a direct descendant of Françoise Guestier, a native of Bordeaux who worked for the Marquis de Segur, owner of Chateau Lafite and Latour. Clos Du Val translates as "small vineyard estate of a small valley," a modest nomenclature for a winery of its stature.

When Goelet, who is also the son of an American entrepreneur, set out on a global search for premium vineyard land, he found the ideal partner in French-born Bernard Portet, a descendant of six generations of winemakers. He followed his passion with formal studies at the French winemaking schools of Toulouse and Montpelier before Goelet hired him in 1970 to help establish Clos Du Val.

Portet spent two years searching six continents before getting a taste of the Napa Valley climate — or, technically, its microclimates. At the time, the cool evenings and dramatic terrain of the Stags Leap District were relatively undiscovered by winemakers. Goelet promptly acquired 150 acres of land in the district. The first vintage of his new venture was a 1972 Cabernet Sauvignon, one of only six California Cabernets selected for the now-legendary Paris tasting in 1976, an event that put the world on notice that Napa Valley was a winemaking force to watch. Ten years later, the same vintage took first place in a rematch, further enhancing Clos Du Val's reputation for creating wines that stand the test of time. In 1973 Goelet purchased 180 acres in another little-recognized appellation—Carneros in southern Napa. Thirteen years later, the winery released its first Carneros Chardonnay, and four years later, its first Carneros Pinot Noir. Today, Goelet's desire to produce wines that express the *terroir* of the vineyards remains the underlying essence of Clos Du Val wines.

A driveway lined with cypress trees leads to the imposing, vine-covered stone winery, behind which the dramatic rock outcroppings of Stags Leap rise in sharp relief. In front of the tasting room are Mediterranean-style gardens, a raised lawn area with tables and chairs defined by a hedge of boxwood, and a demonstration vineyard with twenty rows of Merlot grapevines, accompanied by brief explanations of vineyard management techniques. Inside the winery, halogen lights on the high ceiling beam down on the tasting bar, the unglazed earth-toned tile floor, and a corner display of merchandise bearing the winery's distinctive, curlicued logo. Glass doors on the far side look into a large fermentation room filled with oak and steel tanks. Visitors are welcome to prolong their visit by playing *pétanque* or enjoying a picnic on the lawn or in the olive grove.

DOMAINE CARNEROS

An architectural tribute to its French heritage, the impressive Domaine Carneros château would look at home in Champagne, France. Crowning a hillside in the Carneros region of southern Napa, it is situated in a prime growing area for Chardonnay and Pinot Noir, the primary grape varieties used in sparkling wine. A grand staircase framed by fountains and gardens forms the entrance to the winery. French marble floors, high ceilings, and decorative features such as a Louis XV fireplace mantel impart a palatial ambience. Guests savor wines and food pairings seated at their choice of a private table in the elegant salon, warmed by a fireplace on cool days, or on the broad, sunny terrace with its panoramic views of the surrounding vineyards.

Domaine Carneros started with a quest by Claude Taittinger of Champagne Taittinger in Reims, France, for an ideal site in California for growing and producing world-class sparkling wine. He found it in the Carneros, where a long, moderately cool growing season and breezes from San Pablo Bay allow for slow, even ripening, mature flavors, and bright acidity in Pinot Noir and Chardonnay grapes. Established in 1987, Domaine Carneros now includes five certified organic estate vineyards for a total of 350 acres.

Harvest at Domaine Carneros typically begins in mid-August, when the delicate balance between sugar and acidity is at the optimal point for sparkling wines. Crews head out to pick grapes before dawn, and the fruit is immediately brought to the winery for gentle pressing. Each lot is maintained separately until the perfect blend is determined. At Domaine Carneros, sparkling wines are made in accordance with the rigorous and complex *méthode champenoise*, in which secondary fermentation takes place in the bottle. A growing portfolio of fine Pinot Noir still wines has aficionados of the Burgundian varietal praising the winery's production and the expertise of Pinot Noir winemaker TJ Evans.

Heading this multifaceted operation is founding winemaker/CEO Eileen Crane, who has been with Domaine Carneros from the beginning—helping to locate the winery site and develop the vineyards and facilities. In addition to serving as one of California's pioneering women in wine, Crane has led the way in sustainable grape growing and winemaking. Domaine Carneros became the first sparkling winery in the United States to receive organic certification for 100 percent of its estate vineyards.

DOMAINE CARNEROS
1240 Duhig Rd.
Napa, CA 94559
800-716-BRUT (2788)
707-257-0101
domainecarneros.com

OWNERS: Partnership between Taittinger and Kopf families.

LOCATION: Intersection of Hwys. 121/12 and Duhig Rd., 4 miles southwest of the town of Napa and 6 miles southeast of Sonoma.

APPELLATION: Los Carneros.

HOURS: 10 A.M.–6 P.M. daily.

TASTINGS: $30–$40 for seated tastings (varies by tasting selected); reservations highly recommended. Groups of 8 or more by appointment.

TOURS: 11 A.M., 1 P.M., and 3 P.M. daily. Additional tours offered seasonally. Group tours for 10 or more by appointment.

THE WINES: Brut Rosé, Le Rêve, Pinot Noir, Vintage Brut.

SPECIALTIES: *Méthode champenoise* sparkling wine, Pinot Noir.

WINEMAKERS: Eileen Crane, founding winemaker; TJ Evans, Pinot Noir winemaker.

ANNUAL PRODUCTION: 48,000 cases.

OF SPECIAL NOTE: Table service in salon or on terrace with panoramic views of Carneros region. Cheese and caviar available for purchase.

NEARBY ATTRACTION: di Rosa (indoor and outdoor exhibits of works by contemporary Bay Area artists).

EHLERS ESTATE

EHLERS ESTATE
3222 Ehlers Ln.
St. Helena, CA 94574
707-963-5972
info@ehlersestate.com
ehlersestate.com

OWNER:
Leducq Foundation.

LOCATION: 3 miles north of St. Helena.

APPELLATION: St. Helena.

HOURS: 9:30 A.M.–3:30 P.M. daily.

TASTINGS: $35 for 4 wines, by appointment.

TOURS: None.

THE WINES: Cabernet Franc, Cabernet Sauvignon, Merlot, Petit Verdot, Rosé of Cabernet Franc, Sauvignon Blanc.

SPECIALTIES: 1886 Cabernet Sauvignon, J. Leducq Cabernet Sauvignon.

WINEMAKER:
Kevin Morrisey.

ANNUAL PRODUCTION:
8,000 cases.

OF SPECIAL NOTE: All wines crafted from estate-grown grapes. Certified organic and biodynamic vineyards. Tasting room in restored 1886 stone barn. Picnic area amid century-old olive trees. Bocce ball court. All winery profits benefit the Leducq Foundation, which funds cardiac research.

NEARBY ATTRACTIONS: Culinary Institute of America at Greystone (cooking demonstrations); Bale Grist Mill State Historic Park (water-powered mill circa 1846); Robert Louis Stevenson Museum (author memorabilia).

A stone barn built in 1886 stands tall and sturdy amid the vineyards of Ehlers Estate, named for Bernard Ehlers, the Sacramento grocer who commissioned the structure and planted the olive grove whose trees now shade the winery's sandy picnic area and bocce ball court. The rocky, loamy soils found here at the Napa Valley's narrowest section—what locals call "the pinch" between Spring and Glass mountains—are similar to those found in Rutherford but with a key difference. The microclimate of slightly shorter sun exposure caused by the mountains, along with early-evening winds funneling cold

air through the pinch, produces smooth, lush, and, to aficionados, singular Cabernet Sauvignons. The same holds true for the Ehlers Cabernet Franc and Merlot wines.

Following Ehlers's death in 1901, his wife, Anna, ran the winery for a while, then sold it during Prohibition. Over the years, the property was divided up, and it wasn't until a century after Ehlers's arrival that the potential for success with Bordeaux varietals such as Cabernet Sauvignon was realized. In 1987 the French entrepreneur and philanthropist Jean Leducq, who parlayed his grandfather's Parisian laundry business into what by the late twentieth century reigned as France's largest family-owned company, purchased seven acres once owned by Ehlers. With his wife, Sylviane, he set about reassembling the original Ehlers estate. By 2001, the couple had restored the Ehlers name to the now forty-two-acre property, and their winery had begun gaining recognition for its small-production wines.

The current winemaker, Kevin Morrisey, developed a reputation for making complex, well-balanced wines at Napa Valley's Stags' Leap Winery and Etude in Carneros. Morrisey handcrafts each Ehlers wine from 100 percent organically and biodynamically farmed grapes grown on the estate. Morrisey believes that this style of farming makes possible the degree of agricultural control and deep connection to the land that producing first-rate wines requires.

Seated tastings take place in the remodeled, high-ceiling barn, which may well be the oldest Napa Valley structure in continuous wine-related use. Light streaming in through well-placed windows and wide french doors creates a brighter than expected atmosphere, and the contemporary paintings and plush sofas and chairs play well off nineteenth-century artifacts (among them a wooden wine press) and off the textures of the original stone walls and rough-hewn redwood. The riveted, zinc-topped tasting bar, installed in 2014, tips the balance in favor of modernity, fittingly so given the green direction that the Ehlers winemaking has taken in recent years.

ETUDE WINES

Napa Valley is renowned for its rugged foothills and sun-drenched vineyards, but in its southwestern reaches, visitors find lush, naturally occurring wetlands. Part of the Carneros appellation, this secluded corner supports scores of birds, as well as mature stands of oaks and California bay trees. Here, the marine influence from nearby San Pablo Bay moderates summer heat, helping to extend the growing season for Pinot Noir, Etude's signature wine.

Unlike the sedimentary clay under most Carneros vineyards, the soils of Etude's 1,300-acre property are rocky, well drained, and volcanic, making them ideal for growing Burgundian varieties. Planted to conform  to the changing topography, Etude's vineyard rows run at diverse angles, and blocks average only eight acres. Close spacing of the vines produces low yields of highly flavorful fruit. With four protected wetlands on the property, winery workers take extra care to farm sustainably and keep waterways clean. In fact, having met rigorous standards set by state and federal water quality laws, Etude has received Napa Green and Fish Friendly Farming certification.

Etude Wines was founded in 1982 by winemaker Tony Soter, who believed that improved vineyard practices reduced the need for vinicultural intervention. The winery embraces the philosophy that winemaking begins in the vineyard, and the result is a portfolio of distinguished wines, each expressing authentic varietal characteristics. Etude released its first Napa Valley Cabernet Sauvignon in 1985 and continues to source fruit from prime Cabernet Sauvignon benchlands located throughout Napa Valley. With the release of its first Carneros Pinot Noir, the winery launched its acclaimed Pinot Noir program, which features a six-acre estate vineyard dedicated to rare heirloom selections of the varietal.

In 2005 winemaker Jon Priest moved from the Central Coast to join Etude as winemaker. Priest had worked for more than a dozen years at Wild Horse Winery, where he made upward of thirty varietals, before moving to Adelaida Cellars, and then to TAZ Vineyards, in 2003. He harbors a special fondness for Pinot Noir, savoring the challenges posed by the finicky grape, as well as the pure pleasure it delivers when handled correctly.

In 2009 Etude Wines opened a new tasting room, an elegant space with blond oak paneling and an intricately patterned floor made from end-cut Douglas fir. Embedded rice hulls add a pleasant texture to the concrete tasting bar, and on the wall behind it, a backlit rack holds rows of wine bottles that glow like colorful works of art.

ETUDE WINES
1250 Cuttings Wharf Rd.
Napa, CA 94559
877-586-9361
etudewines.com

LOCATION: About 4 miles southwest of the town of Napa.

APPELLATION: Los Carneros.

HOURS: 10 A.M.–4:30 P.M. daily.

TASTINGS: $15; $25 for reserve wines. $45 for Study of Pinot Noir, 10 A.M., 1 P.M., and 3 P.M., Friday–Sunday, by appointment.

TOURS: None.

THE WINES: Cabernet Sauvignon, Chardonnay, Pinot Blanc, Pinot Gris, Pinot Noir, Rosé of Pinot Noir.

SPECIALTIES: Pinot Noir, Chardonnay, Napa Valley Cabernet.

WINEMAKER: Jon Priest.

ANNUAL PRODUCTION: 28,000 cases.

OF SPECIAL NOTE: Winery is pet friendly. Rutherford, St. Helena, and Oakville Cabernet Sauvignon, Pinot Blanc, and Temblor Pinot Noir sold only in tasting room.

NEARBY ATTRACTION: di Rosa (indoor and outdoor exhibits of works by contemporary Bay Area artists).

FOLEY JOHNSON

FOLEY JOHNSON
8350 St. Helena Hwy.
Rutherford, CA 94573
707-963-1980
info@foleyjohnsonwines
.com
foleyjohnsonwines.com

OWNERS: Bill and Carol
Johnson Foley.

LOCATION: Hwy. 29 between
Oakville and Rutherford.

APPELLATION: Rutherford.

HOURS: 10 A.M.–5 P.M. daily.

TASTINGS: $25 for Estate
tasting of 5 wines; $45
for Handmade Series
reserve tasting of 6 wines,
by appointment; $75 for
Sensory Tasting Seminars
of food paired with the
Handmade wines, by
appointment, with two
days' notice.

TOURS: Estate walking tour
11 A.M.–3 P.M. daily ($45
includes Estate tasting),
preferably by appointment.

THE WINES: Cabernet
Sauvignon, Chardonnay,
Merlot, Sauvignon Blanc.

SPECIALTIES: Handmade
Series of small-production
wines made by Brad
Warner and other Foley
Family Wines winemakers;
Meritage (Cabernet Sauvi-
gnon, Merlot, Petit Verdot,
Cabernet Franc).

WINEMAKER: Brad Warner.

ANNUAL PRODUCTION:
8,000 cases.

OF SPECIAL NOTE: Picnic
area surrounded by vine-
yards; croquet on lawn
behind production facility.

NEARBY ATTRACTIONS: Culinary Institute of America
at Greystone (cooking
demonstrations); Bale
Grist Mill State Historic
Park (water-powered mill
circa 1846); Robert Louis
Stevenson Museum
(author memorabilia).

I t would be imprecise to call a winery along Highway 29 a hidden gem, but there's a touch of that quality to Foley Johnson, a recent Napa arrival ensconced in a proven slice of Cabernet- and Merlot-friendly Rutherford real estate. The winery, whose tasting room occupies a weathered-redwood barn from the 1920s, is named for its owners, Bill and Carol Johnson Foley.

Among the pleasures of a visit to Foley Johnson, which debuted in late 2012, is the chance to sample wines crafted by multiple winemakers at the top of their game. The company's head winemaker, Brad Warner, has five decades of experience making wines in the Napa Valley, including a twenty-nine-year run at the Robert Mondavi Winery, a role in developing the winemaking pro-cesses at prestigious Opus One, and seventeen years at Sawyer Cellars, the prede-cessor winery at the Foley Johnson location. Warner, a genial man with encyclope-dic winemaking knowledge he happily shares with tast-ing room visitors when he's around, crafts all the wines in what Foley Johnson dubs its Estate Bottled and Napa Valley Wines tier. These wines are made from Caber-

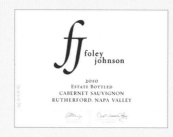

net, Merlot, and other Bordeaux grapes grown on two estate parcels totaling forty-three planted acres, along with fruit from choice vineyards throughout the valley.

Warner also collaborates on a second tier—the smaller-production Handmade Series—with guest winemakers from within the Foley Family Wines group. In addition to Cabernet and other Bordeaux varietals, these wines (sometimes fewer than a hundred cases per selection) include a Napa Valley Zinfandel and a sweet late harvest–style Semillon from Sonoma County fruit. Dave Lattin, the head winemaker at the respected Merus winery in Napa Valley, and Lisa Bishop Forbes of Chalk Hill Estate in Sonoma County are among the talents who have teamed with Warner on Handmade wines.

Estate tastings, which include wines from the first tier, and Handmade Series tastings, with ones from the second tier, take place at a black-granite bar inside the renovated barn. In fine weather, guests also sip out front on a casual patio shaded by orange umbrellas. Bordered by a waist-high flagstone wall, the patio has as its centerpiece a burbling bronze fountain of a gnarled grapevine. Hour-long tours, customized to suit participants' interests, cover the estate's history and its vine-yard, winemaking, and cellaring practices. Included are a visit to the 7,800-square-foot production facility—a 2014 addition whose exterior integrates seamlessly with that of the barn—and an estate tasting in the Library Cellar. The well-conceived Sensory Tasting Seminars address the influence of sight and smell on the wine-tasting process and the interaction between food and wine in the mouth.

FRANCISCAN ESTATE

Water cascades in bubbly waves over the twin tiers of the lotus-shaped stone fountain that anchors the front courtyard of high-profile Franciscan Estate. The fountain is one of several architectural grace notes on this lushly landscaped property that recall California's Spanish mission era.

The winemaking practices at Franciscan were instituted in the mid-1970s by an early proprietor, Justin Meyer, also a cofounder of prestigious Silver Oak Cellars. Around this time, Franciscan purchased prime Oakville acreage whose esteemed neighbors these days include Opus One, Silver Oak, and Harlan Estate. Meyer was a pioneer in farming each vineyard block, or section, according to its soil and microclimate, segregating grapes by block during fermentation and aging, and blending the resulting wines based on the diverse characteristics that emerged. Wineries often abandon such artisanal techniques as case production increases, but Franciscan still considers it vital to making high-quality wines.

Meyer departed after several years, but one of his successors, Agustin Huneeus, now the owner of exclusive Quintessa, introduced Magnificat, Franciscan's signature Bordeaux-style red blend. During Huneeus's tenure, Franciscan also began making a Chardonnay, Cuvée Sauvage, using native yeasts from the vineyard instead of commercial ones. Winemaker since 2003, Janet Myers believes this traditional Burgundian method, rare in California at the time, yields more complex flavors.

Franciscan produces wines from many varietals but at its core remains a Cabernet Sauvignon house, with the Cabernet-predominant Magnificat and five different Cabernets. The Franciscan-owned Mount Veeder Winery in the western Napa Valley hills also makes several Cabernets, providing tasters the opportunity to compare wines using grapes grown on the warmer, loamier valley floor to ones from cooler-climate mountain fruit from rocky soils. At tastings, all-white and all-red flights are possible, and there's a Mount Veeder–only option. Knowledgeable staffers at the main tasting bar, a convivial, high-ceilinged space with light pouring in through a full-length clerestory window, tailor the descriptions of the wines and Franciscan's history to guests' level of interest. On summer weekends, the mood is even more casual at the adjoining outdoor terrace, furnished with tables and chairs, where wines from the tasting bar are also poured. Visitors seeking to delve deeper can reserve a seated private tasting or participate in a blending or other seminar in one of several clubby, dark-paneled rooms furnished with plush leather chairs.

FRANCISCAN ESTATE
1178 Galleron Rd.
St Helena, CA 94574
707-967-3830
info@franciscan.com
franciscan.com

OWNER:
Constellation Brands.

LOCATION: 3 miles south of downtown St. Helena.

APPELLATIONS: Oakville, Mt. Veeder, Los Carneros.

HOURS: 10 A.M.–5 P.M. daily.

TASTINGS: $15–$25 for 4–6 wines; $15–$25 for 4–6 current-release, small-production, or reserve wines.

TOURS: Vineyard and barrel tours (including tastings), by appointment.

THE WINES: Cabernet Sauvignon, Chardonnay, Merlot, Port, Rosé of Syrah, Sauvignon Blanc.

SPECIALTIES: Equilibrium and Fountain Court white blends, Franciscan Oakville Estate Cabernet Sauvignon, Magnificat red blend, Mount Veeder Cabernet Franc and Cabernet Sauvignon.

WINEMAKER: Janet Myers.

ANNUAL PRODUCTION: 280,000 cases.

OF SPECIAL NOTE: Rose garden area for picnics. Tastings include wines from Mount Veeder Winery. Franciscan Estate Reserve Lunch with wine pairing (Fridays). Blending and sensory seminars by reservation. Events include Mount Veeder release party (April), Magnificat release party (July), Harvest Party Grape Stomp (October). Twelve small-production wines available only in tasting room.

NEARBY ATTRACTION: Culinary Institute of America at Greystone (cooking demonstrations).

47

FRANK FAMILY VINEYARDS

FRANK FAMILY VINEYARDS
1091 Larkmead Ln.
Calistoga, CA 94515
800-574-9463
info@frankfamily
vineyards.com
frankfamilyvineyards.com

OWNERS:
Rich and Leslie Frank.

LOCATION: About 5 miles
north of downtown
St. Helena via Hwy. 29.

APPELLATION: Napa Valley.

HOURS: 10 A.M.–5 P.M. daily.

TASTINGS: $20 for 4 wines;
$30 for sparkling wine and
reserve wines. Reservations
suggested.

TOURS: None.

THE WINES: Cabernet
Sauvignon, Chardonnay,
late-harvest Chardonnay,
Petite Sirah, Pinot Noir,
Port, Sangiovese, sparkling
wine, Zinfandel.

SPECIALTIES: Cabernet
Sauvignon from Ruth-
erford, sparkling wine,
Chardonnay.

WINEMAKER: Todd Graff.

ANNUAL PRODUCTION:
100,000 cases.

OF SPECIAL NOTE: Picnic
tables for use by visitors.
Reserve Lewis Chardon-
nay, Pinot Noir, Sangio-
vese, and Zinfandel;
Rutherford Reserve
Cabernet; Winston Hill
Red Wine; and *méthode
champenoise* wines avail-
able only at winery.

NEARBY ATTRACTIONS:
Bothe-Napa State Park;
Robert Louis Stevenson
State Park; Old Faithful
Geyser of California; Petri-
fied Forest; Sharpsteen
Museum (exhibits on
Robert Louis Stevenson
and Walt Disney animator
Ben Sharpsteen).

At a time when many Napa Valley wineries are increasingly exclusive, the convivial, unpretentious ambience at Frank Family Vineyards is decidedly refreshing. Yet this is not the only reason for heading slightly off the beaten path to reach this historic property. Frank Family Vineyards is home to a massive stone building constructed in 1884 as Larkmead Winery, the third oldest winery in Napa. Refurbished in 1906 with sandstone from the nearby hills, the structure is listed on the National Register of Historic Places and as an official Point of Historical Interest in the state of California.

In 1990 Rich Frank purchased a home and property in Rutherford as an easy getaway destination from the hustle and bustle of Hollywood during his tenure as president of Disney Studios. With a great hillside vineyard, Winston Hill, already in his portfolio, in 1992 he purchased the historic stone winery. He then slowly started to build production by acquiring several additional vineyards in the Napa Valley, including the Wood's Ranch Vineyard in Rutherford, the Lewis Vineyard in the Carneros, and the S&J Vineyard in Capell Valley. Today the winery owns nearly three hundred acres of vineyards, which winemaker Todd Graff utilizes to produce Frank's wines. While the winery has been credited with leading the grower-producer sparkling wine movement in California, the focus at Frank Family Vineyards is largely on still wines. Driving Frank Family's acclaim are three distinct Cabernets and Cabernet blends: the Napa Valley Cabernet, the Rutherford Reserve Cabernet, and Winston Hill. The winery also produces very small quantities of vineyard-designated wines. Carneros Chardonnay is Frank Family's most popular bottling in the United States.

Rich, along with his wife, Leslie, an Emmy Award–winning TV journalist, knows how to make visitors feel welcome. The tasting room, at times brimming with laughter, has been recognized consistently among the best in Napa in Bay Area polls. It has also received critical recognition as *Connoisseurs' Guide to California Wine* "Winery of the Year" and top rankings in the *Wine & Spirits* annual restaurant poll.

Visitors to the tasting room have the option to taste both still and sparkling wines in one of six tasting areas in the yellow Craftsman house. They may also enjoy the grounds, including the picnic tables under the towering elm trees on the property, or the rocking chairs on the front porch. The luckiest guests may even receive a warm welcome from one of the winery's dogs—Riley, a German shepherd, or Bristol, a chocolate lab.

GRGICH HILLS ESTATE

F ew people driving along Highway 29 recognize both of the red, white, and blue flags flying in front of this winery. They certainly know one, the American flag. The other represents Croatia, the native country of winemaker and co-owner Miljenko "Mike" Grgich.

The simple red-tile-roofed, white stucco building may not be as flashy as those of nearby wineries, but as the saying goes, it's what's inside that counts. Once visitors pass beneath the grapevine trellis and into the dimly lit recesses of the tasting room, they forget about exterior appearances. The comfortable, old-world atmosphere at Grgich Hills Estate is not a gimmick.

The winery was founded by Mike Grgich (pronounced "GUR-gitch") and Austin E. Hills on July 4, 1977. Both were already of the Hills Brothers coffee legendary, especially in France. attention in 1976, when, at the all-French panel of judges telena Chardonnay over the in a blind tasting. It was a California wine industry in

well known. Hills is a member family. Grgich was virtually He had drawn worldwide now-famous Paris tasting, an chose his 1973 Chateau Mon- best of the white Burgundies momentous occasion for the general and in particular for

Mike Grgich, who was already acknowledged as one of the state's top winemakers.

Finally in a position to capitalize on his fame, Grgich quickly found a simpatico partner in Hills, who had a background in business and finance and was the owner of established vineyards. The two men shortly began turning out the intensely flavored Chardonnays that remain the flagship wines of Grgich Hills Estate.

Grgich, easily recognizable with his trademark blue beret, was born in 1923 into a winemaking family on the Dalmatian coast of Croatia. He arrived in California in 1958 and spent his early years at Beaulieu Vineyard, where he worked with the late, pioneering winemaker André Tchelistcheff before moving on to Mondavi and Chateau Montelena. Grgich continues to make wine and relies on a younger generation—daughter Violet Grgich, vice president of sales and marketing, and nephew Ivo Jeramaz, vice president of production and vineyard development—to carry on the family tradition. Visitors may well run into family members when taking the exceptionally informative winery tour or while sampling wines in the cool, cellarlike tasting room or in the VIP tasting room and hospitality center.

GRGICH HILLS ESTATE
1829 St. Helena Hwy.
Rutherford, CA 94573
800-532-3057
info@grgich.com
grgich.com

OWNERS: Miljenko "Mike" Grgich and Austin Hills.

LOCATION: About 3 miles south of St. Helena.

APPELLATION: Napa Valley.

HOURS: 9:30 A.M.–4:30 P.M. daily.

TASTINGS: $20 for 5 wines.

TOURS: By appointment, 11 A.M. and 2 P.M. daily.

THE WINES: Cabernet Sauvignon, Chardonnay, Fumé Blanc, Merlot, Violetta (late-harvest dessert wine), Zinfandel.

SPECIALTY: Chardonnay.

WINEMAKER: Mike Grgich.

ANNUAL PRODUCTION: 65,000 cases.

OF SPECIAL NOTE: Barrel tastings held 2–4 P.M. on Friday afternoons November–May. Grape stomping offered daily during harvest. Napa Valley Wine Train stops at Grgich Hills for special tour and tasting; call 800-427-4124 for schedule.

NEARBY ATTRACTIONS: Bothe-Napa State Park (hiking, picnicking, horseback riding, swimming Memorial Day–Labor Day); Bale Grist Mill State Historic Park (waterpowered mill circa 1846); Robert Louis Stevenson Museum (author memorabilia).

HALL ST. HELENA

HALL ST. HELENA
401 St. Helena Hwy. South
St. Helena, CA 94574
707-967-2626
800-688-4255
hospitality@hallwines.com
hallwines.com

OWNERS: Kathryn Walt Hall and Craig Hall.

LOCATION: 1.5 miles south of downtown St. Helena.

APPELLATION: St. Helena.

HOURS: 10 A.M.–5:30 P.M. daily.

TASTINGS: $30 for 4 wines.

TOURS: Daily on the hour by appointment (walk-ins possible).

THE WINES: Cabernet Sauvignon, Merlot, Sauvignon Blanc, Syrah.

SPECIALTIES: Cabernet Sauvignon, Craig's Cuvée (Cabernet Sauvignon, Merlot, Syrah), Darwin (Syrah).

WINEMAKER: Steve Leveque.

ANNUAL PRODUCTION: 70,000 cases.

OF SPECIAL NOTE: Winery displays owners' collection of contemporary art. Gold LEED-certified winery; pet friendly in outdoor spaces. Events include Cabernet Cook Off (May) and Kathryn Hall Cabernet Sauvignon Release Party (September). Special tours and tastings for a fee include Wine Tasting 101 and Demystifying Wine and Food. Wines from sister winery Walt available for tasting. A second winery, Hall Rutherford, is open only by appointment. Many wines available only in tasting room.

NEARBY ATTRACTIONS: Culinary Institute of America at Greystone (cooking demonstrations); Robert Louis Stevenson Museum (author memorabilia).

A thirty-five-foot polished stainless steel sculpture of a leaping rabbit draws immediate attention to the entrance of Hall St. Helena. Often gleaming in the midday sun, the piece is at once flamboyant, elegant, and meticulously crafted, a description that applies equally well to the wines produced by this state-of-the-art winery. As frequently occurs with owners Kathryn and Craig Hall, a good story lies behind this artwork they commissioned from Lawrence Argent: it's named *Bunny Foo Foo* after the high-spirited title character in a poem that Kathryn's children recited at the Mendocino County vineyard her parents established in the 1970s.

Kathryn managed her family's vineyard for a decade, but shortly after relinquishing that role longed to return to the wine business. By then she was living in Dallas and married to Craig, the founder and chairman of Hall Financial Group. (Another good story: Ann Richards, the quick-witted late Texas governor, played the couple's matchmaker.) The Halls eventually purchased a property now known as Hall Rutherford, whose hillside Sacrashe Vineyard is among the Napa Valley's elite Cabernet grow-ing spots. Before they could begin making wine in earnest, though, President Bill Clinton appointed Kathryn U.S. ambassador to Austria, a post she held from 1997 to 2001.

Upon returning to California, the Halls assembled an experienced winery team, bought the St. Helena property, and set out to create high-end Cabernet Sauvignon wines. Within a half decade, one had achieved a top ranking from *Wine Enthusiast* magazine, and another had placed high on *Wine Spectator*'s Top 100 list. Under the current winemaker, Steve Leveque, the wines continue to earn stellar ratings. Leveque, a trained viticulturist who can often be found inspecting Hall's vines, attributes the winery's consistent success to shrewdly selected vineyards — a recent Cabernet boasted fruit from thirteen of the Napa Valley's sixteen appellations — and "no excuses" perfectionism.

For visitors, the attention to detail first manifests itself in architect Jarrod Denton's dramatic glass-walled visitor center, an environmentally friendly structure that opened in 2013, and in outdoor artworks such as Patrick Dougherty's *Deck the Halls*, a beguiling series of nest-like, walk-through lairs assembled from willow saplings. Tastings occur in Gallery 401, a large, light-filled space with vineyard and mountain views and in smaller, private tasting rooms nearby. A tasting might begin with Hall Sauvignon Blanc and a Chardonnay and a Pinot Noir from sister winery Walt Wines in downtown Sonoma, followed by some Cabernets. Tours focus on the Halls' art collection and the history of the St. Helena property, where wine has been made since the 1870s.

Heitz Wine Cellars

In 1961, when Joe and Alice Heitz produced their first bottle of wine, they never dreamed that one day Heitz wines would grace dining tables across the country and even around the world. The couple started Heitz Wine Cellars on an eight-acre vineyard just south of St. Helena when Napa Valley had fewer than twenty wineries. As news spread about the quality of the wines, their business grew. In 1964 the Heitzes acquired 160 acres of pristine farmland in the gently sloping hills near the Silverado Trail. This property, which included an historic stone cellar built in 1898, became the heart of their family business.

Two of their earliest visitors were Tom and Martha May, owners of Martha's Vineyard in Oakville. The Heitzes agreed to purchase their fruit, and when Joe Heitz crafted an especially remarkable 1966 vintage, the two families decided to put the vineyard's name on the bottle, creating the vineyard designation. Martha's is now one of the most widely recognized wines in the world, and the Heitz family's exclusive arrangement to produce wine grapes continues today. Heitz from the Martha's Vineyard Trailside Vineyard and Napa Valley Cabernets have also earned acclaim.

Joe Heitz was a founder of the "new" winery movement. Believing that Napa Valley wines could compete on the world stage, he took the lead in pursuing quality and commanding prices that reflected greater parity with European wines. The Heitz family was also among the first to export their wines. Offering fresh insights and taking bold steps earned Heitz the admiration of generations of California winemakers, as well as induction in 2012 into the Hall of Fame at the Culinary Institute of America.

The second generation now leads the family business. President Kathleen Heitz Myers and winemaker David Heitz have made their mark by skillfully balancing innovative business practices and signature winemaking traditions. Myers carries on the family legacy of leadership in the wine industry, having served as chair of the California Wine Institute board of directors and as president of the Napa Valley Vintners. In 2002, at the site of the original winery, the family built a new sales and tasting room of native stone. On a back patio, visitors can admire panoramic views within feet of the first Cabernet Sauvignon vines. As the Heitzes celebrate the milestone of their fifty-fourth anniversary, a third generation has joined the business. Heitz Wine Cellars is one of the few wineries established during the renaissance of Napa Valley winemaking to remain family owned.

HEITZ WINE CELLARS
TASTING AND SALES ROOM:
436 St. Helena Hwy. South
St. Helena, CA 94574
707-963-3542

MAILING ADDRESS:
500 Taplin Rd.
St. Helena, CA 94574
heitzcellar.com

OWNERS: Heitz family.

LOCATION: 2 miles south of St. Helena.

APPELLATION: Napa Valley.

HOURS: 11 A.M.–4:30 P.M. daily.

TASTINGS: Complimentary.

TOURS: Of winery by appointment.

THE WINES: Cabernet Sauvignon, Chardonnay, Grignolino, Port, Sauvignon Blanc, Zinfandel.

SPECIALTY: Vineyard-designated Cabernet Sauvignon.

WINEMAKER: David Heitz.

ANNUAL PRODUCTION: 40,000 cases.

OF SPECIAL NOTE: Most vineyards certified organic. The only Napa Valley producer of Grignolino, a red Italian wine grape commonly grown in the Piedmont region.

NEARBY ATTRACTIONS: Culinary Institute of America at Greystone (cooking demonstrations); Bothe-Napa State Park (hiking, picnicking, horseback riding, swimming Memorial Day–Labor Day); Bale Grist Mill State Historic Park (water-powered mill circa 1846); Robert Louis Stevenson Museum (author memorabilia).

THE HESS COLLECTION WINERY

THE HESS COLLECTION WINERY
4411 Redwood Rd.
Napa, CA 94558
707-255-8584
hesscollection.com

FOUNDER: Donald Hess.

LOCATION: 7 miles west of Hwy. 29.

APPELLATIONS: Mt. Veeder, Napa Valley.

HOURS: 10 A.M.–5:30 P.M. daily.

TASTINGS: $20–$50. Various food-and-wine pairings ($30–$85) offered daily by reservation.

TOURS: Art collection open daily; museum admission is free. Guided tours of winery and collection available.

THE WINES: Cabernet Sauvignon, Chardonnay, Malbec, 19 Block Cuvée, Sauvignon Blanc, Viognier, Zinfandel.

SPECIALTIES: Mount Veeder Cabernet Sauvignon, Chardonnay, 19 Block Cuvée.

WINEMAKERS: David Guffy (Hess), Randle Johnson (Artezin).

ANNUAL PRODUCTION: Unavailable.

OF SPECIAL NOTE: Extensive collection of contemporary art. Many wines available only in tasting room.

NEARBY ATTRACTIONS: di Rosa (indoor and outdoor exhibits of works by contemporary artists); Alston Regional Park (hiking).

A gently winding road heads up a forested mountainside to this winery on the western rim of the Napa Valley. Although only a fifteen-minute drive from bustling Highway 29, the estate feels a thousand times removed. Arriving visitors are greeted with stunning vineyard views from almost every vantage point.

Swiss entrepreneur Donald Hess has owned vineyards on Mount Veeder since 1978, so when he decided to establish his own winery, he didn't have to look far to find the Christian Brothers Mont La Salle property. He already knew that the east side of the extinct volcano provides a cool climate that allows a long growing season as well as excellent soil drainage—two viticultural components

known for producing Cabernet Sauvignon with excellent structure and superb concentration of aromas and flavors. Vineyards were first planted on this land in the 1860s, long before the ivy-clad, three-story stone winery was built in 1903. The Christian Brothers produced wine here for nearly a half century before leasing the facilities to Hess in 1986. He began planting Cabernet Sauvignon vineyards on terrain so steep they have to be picked by hand. The vines must grow extended roots to cling to the mountainside, and the resultant stress creates fruit of exceptional character.

The Hess Collection farms 310 acres of Mount Veeder vineyards that range in elevation from six hundred to two thousand feet. Viewing itself as a steward of the land, the winery farms these vineyards using the principles of sustainable and organic agriculture. The vineyards and winery have been certified by the Napa Green program of the Napa Valley Vintners.

Hess spent three years renovating the facility before opening it to the public in 1989. The overhaul included transforming 13,000 square feet on the second and third floors to display his extensive collection of international art, which consists of 143 paintings, sculptures, and interactive pieces by modern and contemporary artists, among them such luminaries as Francis Bacon, Frank Stella, Anselm Kiefer, Andy Goldsworthy, and Robert Motherwell. One work evokes a particularly strong response for its social commentary. It is Argentinean Leopold Maler's *Hommage 1974*, an eternally burning typewriter created in protest of the repression of artistic freedom.

The tasting room, which shares the first floor with a century-old barrel-aging cellar, is built from a local iron-rich limestone quarried from the property. The stone had been covered with stucco by the Christian Brothers but was inadvertently exposed during the winery's renovation. This is where visitors linger and share their impressions of both the wine and the art.

INGLENOOK

Inglenook was founded in 1879 by Finnish sea captain Gustave Niebaum, who made his fortune in the Alaska fur trade. He modeled the massive stone château after the estates he had visited in Bordeaux and imported the best European grapevines to plant nearby. By the time Francis and Eleanor Coppola entered the picture nearly a century later, however, a series of corporate ownerships had divided the estate and damaged its brand.

Seeking a weekend home in wine country, the Coppolas were shown the historic Niebaum mansion in 1975, the start of their thirty-five-year journey to restore the original estate and its label. By 1995, the Coppolas had acquired the major parcels of the original estate and renamed it Niebaum-Coppola. They replanted vineyards with the same type of rootstock origi-nally used by the founder in the 1800s and began bringing the château and its grounds back to their former glory. The European-style front courtyard now features a redwood and stone pergola graced with grapevines and a ninety-by-thirty-foot reflect-ing pool that is illuminated at night. In the vaulted entrance is another of Francis Coppola's most dramatic creations: a grand staircase built of exotic hardwoods imported from

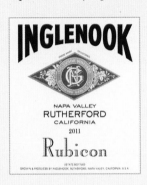

Belize. The château also includes an exhibit celebrating milestones in Inglenook's long, illustri-ous history, including the production of the 1941 Cabernet Sauvignon, heralded as one of the greatest wines ever made.

When Coppola set out to craft a proprietary red wine using the acclaimed estate vineyards in 1978, he decided to call it Rubicon, signifying the point of no return. The Bordeaux-style blend remains the winery's premier red wine. In 2011 Coppola acquired the iconic Inglenook trademark, restoring the estate's original name. At the same time, Philippe Bascaules, renowned winemaker from Bordeaux, France, came on board.

Visitors may take part in one of three daily programs, a ninety-minute tour, and a seated tast-ing with food accompaniments. Those seeking to learn even more may opt for the Elevage Experi-ence. This detailed look at winemaking, emphasizing the flagship wine Rubicon, ends with barrel samples paired with artisan cheese in the caves. Inglenook also offers personalized private tours and tastings.

INGLENOOK
1991 St. Helena Hwy.
Rutherford, CA 94573
707-968-1161
800-782-4266
reservations@inglenook.com
inglenook.com

OWNERS: Francis and Eleanor Coppola.

LOCATION: About 3 miles south of St. Helena.

APPELLATIONS: Rutherford, Napa Valley.

HOURS: Château: 11 A.M.–5 P.M. daily. Bistro: 10 A.M.–5 P.M. daily.

TASTINGS: $50 for sit-down tasting of 4 estate wines. Reservations required.

TOURS: 11 A.M., 1:30 P.M., and 3 P.M. daily. Reservations required (707-968-1161).

THE WINES: Blancaneaux (white blend), CASK Cabernet Sauvignon, Edizione Pennino Zinfandel, RC Reserve Syrah, Rubicon (premier red blend).

SPECIALTY: Rubicon.

WINEMAKER: Philippe Bascaules.

ANNUAL PRODUCTION: Unavailable.

OF SPECIAL NOTE: Extensive shop with estate olive oil, books, wine accessories, and gifts. More than 200 acres of organically certified vineyards. Wines by the glass, espresso, sodas, and light snacks offered at the Bistro Wine Bar.

NEARBY ATTRACTIONS: Robert Louis Stevenson Museum (author memorabilia); Napa Valley Museum (winemaking displays, art exhibits); Culinary Institute of America at Greystone (cooking demonstrations).

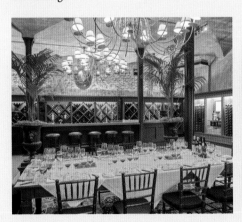

MUMM NAPA

MUMM NAPA
8445 Silverado Trail
Rutherford, CA 94573
707-967-7700
mumm_info@mumm
napa.com
mummnapa.com

OWNER: Pernod Ricard USA.

LOCATION: East of
Rutherford, 1 mile south
of Rutherford Cross Rd.

APPELLATION: Napa Valley.

HOURS: 10 A.M.–5 P.M. daily
(last seating at 4:45 P.M.).

TASTINGS: $18 and up for
flights, or $10 and up by
the flute.

TOURS: 11 A.M., 1 P.M., and
3 P.M. daily.

THE WINES: Blanc de Blancs,
Brut Prestige, Brut Reserve,
Brut Rosé, Demi-Sec, DVX,
Sparkling Pinot Noir.

SPECIALTIES: Sparkling wine
made in traditional French
style; Devaux Ranch single-
vineyard estate sparkling
wine.

WINEMAKER:
Ludovic Dervin.

ANNUAL PRODUCTION:
250,000 cases.

OF SPECIAL NOTE: Collection
of Ansel Adams photography
and exhibitions of works by
renowned photographers
(free admission). Majority
of wines available only at
winery. Limited availability
of large-format bottles at
winery.

NEARBY ATTRACTION:
Napa Valley Museum
(winemaking displays,
art exhibits).

For connoisseurs of Champagne, relaxing outdoors on a sunny day with a glass of bubbly, in the company of good friends, taking in a panoramic vineyard view, may be the ultimate pleasure. This is obviously what Champagne Mumm of France had in mind when in 1979 it dispatched the late Guy Devaux to North America to establish a winery that could develop a sparkling wine that would live up to Champagne standards.

Devaux, a native of Epernay, the epicenter of France's Champagne district, was an expert on *méthode champenoise*. In  this French style of wine-making, the wine under-goes its bubble-producing fermentation in the very bottle from which it will be poured. After crisscrossing the United States for four years conducting research, Devaux decreed the Napa Valley, with its varied soils and hot summer days and cool evenings and early mornings, the locale most capable of producing grapes with the acidity required of distinguished sparkling wines.

As founding winemaker, Devaux established the house style of blending wines from numerous sources, and his current successor, Ludovic Dervin, continues the tradition. Mumm Napa prides itself on its relationships with more than fifty noteworthy growers, some of whom have been farming for five generations. Dervin, a Champagne native with experience at wineries in both France and California, blends wines made from individual grape lots to create widely distributed offerings such as Mumm's signature Brut Prestige and rarer ones that include the vintage-dated series DVX—Devaux's name minus the vowels. Mumm also honored Devaux by naming its sole single-vineyard bottling, Devaux Ranch, after him, along with the Carneros site where the wine's Chardonnay, Pinot Noir, and Pinot Meunier grapes are grown.

DVX wines—equal parts Chardonnay and Pinot Noir—are the centerpiece of seated Oak Terrace tastings, shaded by large crimson umbrellas and the outstretched branches of a nearly two-century-old blue oak tree. A plate of cheeses, nuts, and fresh and dried fruit accompanies the wines. Flights and wines by the glass are poured in the light-filled salon and on the adjoining open-air patio. Mumm's tours cover the sparkling winemaking process, including grape varietals and vineyard management, fermentation, blending, bottling, aging, and *dosage*, the process of adding wine mixed with pure sugar to create the requisite residual sugar level for the type of wine (drier or sweeter) being made. Tours conclude at Mumm's photography gallery, which displays twenty-seven original Ansel Adams prints and presents exhibitions of other well-regarded photographers' works.

PEJU

Spotting Peju, even on a winery-lined stretch of Highway 29, is easy, thanks to a fifty-foot-tall tasting tower topped with a distinctive copper roof. Although the tasting tower opened only in late 2003, the structure looks as if it has been there for decades. Like the rest of the property, it could have been transplanted directly from the countryside of southern France.

The Rutherford estate had been producing wine grapes for more than eighty years when Anthony and Herta Peju bought it in 1983. The couple has been improving the thirty-acre property ever since, honing vineyard techniques and adding Merlot and Cabernet Franc grapes to

the estate's core product, Cabernet Sauvignon. By the mid-1990s, demand for Peju wines outstripped the winery's supply. To satisfy it, the Pejus acquired a 350-acre property in northern Napa County in Pope Valley, planted a variety of grapes, and named it Persephone Vineyard, after a goddess in Greek mythology.

Anthony Peju had been living in Europe when he was lured by the movie industry to Los Angeles, where he met Herta Behensky, his future wife. Peju established his own nursery, but had long dreamed of owning a farm. The vibrant towns in Napa Valley and their proximity to San Francisco motivated him to begin a search for vineyard property that ended two years later with the acquisition of what would become Peju Province Winery.

Peju's horticultural experience, combined with his wife's talent for gardening, resulted in two acres of immaculately kept winery gardens. Together, they established a dramatic series of outdoor rooms linked by footpaths and punctuated with fountains and marble sculpture. Hundreds of flowering plants and trees create an aromatic retreat for the Pejus and their visitors. Lining both sides of the driveway are forty-foot-tall sycamore trees, their trunks adorned by gnarled spirals. Visitors reach the tasting room by crossing a small bridge over a pool with fountains. An entrance door of Brazilian cherrywood opens onto a naturally lighted room where three muses grace a century-old stained-glass window.

After more than thirty years, Peju remains a small, family-owned winery with two generations working together. Since 2001, elder daughter Lisa has traveled the world representing Peju wines and reaching out to younger customers. Ariana, who joined the team in 2006, has spearheaded such environmental initiatives as installing enough solar panels to provide 40 percent of the energy for the winery (now a Napa Green Certified Winery), earning organic certification at Peju's Rutherford estate, and practicing sustainable farming at the winery's other two properties.

PEJU
8466 St. Helena Hwy.
(Hwy. 29)
Rutherford, CA 94573
707-963-3600
800-446-7358
info@peju.com
peju.com

OWNERS: Anthony and Herta Peju.

LOCATION: 11 miles north of the town of Napa.

APPELLATIONS: Rutherford, Napa Valley.

HOURS: 10 A.M.–6 P.M. daily.

TASTINGS: $25.

TOURS: Self-guided or by appointment.

THE WINES: Cabernet Franc, Cabernet Sauvignon, Chardonnay, Merlot, Petit Verdot, Provence, Sauvignon Blanc, Syrah, Zinfandel.

SPECIALTIES: Reserve Cabernet Sauvignon, H.B. Vineyard Cabernet Sauvignon, Fifty/fifty (Bordeaux blend).

WINEMAKER: Sara Fowler.

ANNUAL PRODUCTION: 35,000 cases.

OF SPECIAL NOTE: Wine-and-food pairings, cooking classes, gift boutique. Barrel tasting by reservation. Art gallery featuring work by contemporary artists. Many wines available only at winery.

NEARBY ATTRACTIONS: Robert Louis Stevenson Museum (author memorabilia); Napa Valley Museum (winemaking displays, art exhibits); Culinary Institute of America at Greystone (cooking demonstrations).

PROVENANCE AND HEWITT VINEYARDS

PROVENANCE AND HEWITT VINEYARDS
1695 St. Helena Hwy.
Rutherford, CA 94573
707-968-3638
866-253-4456
info@hewittvineyard.com
hewittvineyard.com

OWNER: Diageo Chateau and Estate Wines.

LOCATION: 1 mile north of downtown Rutherford.

APPELLATION: Rutherford.

HOURS: 10 A.M.–5 P.M. daily.

TASTINGS: $25 for Provenance Premier Tasting of 4 or 5 wines; $30 for Provenance Reserve Tasting of 5 wines; $55 for Hewitt Reserve Tasting of 5 wines, by appointment.

TOURS: 11 A.M. and 3:30 P.M. ($35), appointment recommended.

THE WINES: Cabernet Franc, Cabernet Sauvignon, Malbec, Merlot, Muscat, Port, Rosé of Malbec, Sauvignon Blanc.

SPECIALTIES: Hewitt Cabernet Sauvignon, Provenance Winemaker's Reserve red blend.

WINEMAKER: Chris Cooney.

ANNUAL PRODUCTION: 55,000 cases (Provenance); 3,900 cases (Hewitt).

OF SPECIAL NOTE: Tasting patio out front. Harvest Grape Stomp Luncheon (August); Black Friday Weekend Cellar Sale (November). All Hewitt wines and most Provenance wines available only in tasting room.

NEARBY ATTRACTIONS: Culinary Institute of America at Greystone (cooking demonstrations); Bale Grist Mill State Historic Park (water-powered mill circa 1846); Robert Louis Stevenson Museum (author memorabilia).

A sprawling wine-red winery backed by the Mayacamas Mountains catches the eye along its stretch of Highway 29 in the Rutherford appellation's northern section. The sun here shines brilliantly, highlighting tightly spaced, light green rows of Sauvignon Blanc and Semillon grapevines extending westward from the railroad tracks that parallel the highway to the mountains' greener, forested foothills.

The Sauvignon Blanc, its fruit more concentrated because of the vine spacing, is often the first wine poured in the Provenance tasting room. Light streaming through the room's arched windows reflects off the highly polished floor, made from the staves of the oak barrels—complete with their coopers' marks—used  to age the winery's first (1999) vintage. As the building's color suggests, a visit to Provenance is mostly about reds, more than half of which are Cabernet Sauvignons made from grapes sourced from notable Rutherford and Oakville vineyards. Hewitt Vineyards, a sister winery with a small, appointment-only tasting room off the main Provenance space, releases a single Cabernet Sauvignon each year from estate grapes grown west of the Sauvignon Blanc. The fifty-seven-acre Hewitt vineyard produces distinguished Cabernets year after year, wines that became all the more coveted after *Wine Spectator* magazine ranked the 2010 vintage the number four wine worldwide.

Chris Cooney oversees production of both labels. A graduate of the U.C. Davis winemaking program with an affinity for biology and chemistry, Cooney embraces the latest advances in viticultural science and technology. Aerial photography and computer graphics, for instance, allow him and vineyard crews to analyze rows vine by vine to diagnose weak spots and make watering, leaf-pruning, and other adjustments. Come harvesttime, though, Cooney's methods turn strictly old-school: he decides when to pick the grapes by how they taste and opts for a rigorous hand-sorting regime to remove stems, overripe grapes, and other unwanted material before fermentation.

Some of the activities of Cooney and his wine-cellar crew can be observed through a large semicircular window at the rear of the tasting room. When the workers open the cellar's back doors, the cameo view of the estate vineyards behind them extends back to the Mayacamas. In mid-2014 the winery opened an instantly popular outdoor lounge out front that has views east to the Vaca Range. Shaded by umbrellas and seated on comfortable patio furniture, lounge guests can enjoy one of the Provenance tastings or purchase wines to sip by the glass or the bottle.

RAYMOND VINEYARDS

RAYMOND VINEYARDS
849 Zinfandel Ln.
St. Helena, CA 94574
707-963-3141
customerservice@
raymondvineyards.com
raymondvineyards.com

OWNER:
Boisset Collection.

LOCATION: 2 miles southeast
of St. Helena.

APPELLATION: Rutherford.

HOURS: 10 A.M.–4 P.M. daily.

TASTINGS: $20 for 5 current
releases; $25 for 5 Crystal
Cellar District Cabernet
Sauvignons.

TOURS: $40, includes
Theater of Nature, Crystal
Cellar, and sit-down tasting
of 6 wines. Reservations
required 24 hours in
advance.

THE WINES: Cabernet
Sauvignon, Chardonnay,
Merlot, Sauvignon Blanc.

SPECIALTY: Generations
(Cabernet Sauvignon).

WINEMAKER:
Stephanie Putnam.

ANNUAL PRODUCTION:
200,000 cases.

OF SPECIAL NOTE: Classes on
winemaking, wine-and-
food pairing, and blending
wines by appointment.
Private library tastings by
appointment. Two-acre
demonstration garden with
self-guided tour using on-
site signage or smartphone
audio. Bocce ball court.
Small Lot Collection available only in tasting room.

NEARBY ATTRACTIONS: Bothe-
Napa State Park (hiking,
picnicking, horseback riding, swimming Memorial
Day–Labor Day); Robert
Louis Stevenson Museum
(author memorabilia).

A fantasyland of oenological pleasures awaits visitors who venture inside the ranch-style complex at Raymond Vineyards. With the first glimpse of the dazzling Crystal Cellar, tasters know they've discovered a unique world of sensory surprises, delivered amid dancing neon lights and surreal decor. Entered via a doorway lit by a luminous hologram of a crystal vase, the Crystal Cellar is a working winery, complete with fermentation tanks and a second-story catwalk. When open for tasting, however, the ambience shifts to that of a chic nightclub glittering with candles, Baccarat crystal chandeliers, and dramatic gleams bouncing off the stainless steel walls and mirror-lined bar. Leggy mannequins clad in faux-fur bikinis pose on the catwalk and dangle from a trapeze with saucy abandon. Servers pouring single-vineyard Cab- ernet Sauvignon from crystal decanters demonstrate how aeration smooths and softens young red wines by integrating aroma, texture, and flavor. The wild, yet muted lighting creates a magical effect and encourages tasters to rely upon their senses of smell and taste— rather than sight—to experi- ence the wine.

In a side room fitted with reflective stainless steel walls and a spinning mirrored ball, instructional blending sessions take place by appointment. Called the Blend-ing Room, it resembles a spaceship version of a high-tech laboratory. Visitors don futuristic silver lab coats to play mad scientists, and after crafting the perfect Napa Valley blend, they create custom labels for the bottles they will take home. Down the hall, a peek into the members-only Red Room reveals a plush lair decorated in multiple shades of red representing the colors of Cabernet Sauvignon.

Jean-Charles Boisset, whose Boisset Family Estates purchased the winery in 2009, has created a wine lover's playground with a series of interactive attractions. His fun-loving personality is evident throughout the estate and shines in such features as Frenchie Winery, a deluxe five-bed kennel for visiting dogs, and the oversized thronelike chairs set about the lawn for visiting humans. A native of France, Boisset farms his family's Burgundian vineyards using biodynamic practices that empha-size the interplay of soils, plants, and animals. He implemented biodynamic farming at Raymond Vineyards in 2010, when he replanted one-third of the estate's original eighty-one-acre vineyard. The entire ninety-acre estate is farmed according to biodynamic practices and was certified by Demeter in 2013. To illustrate the benefits of this farming method, Boisset created a two-acre demonstration garden called the Theater of Nature. White canvas curtains billow at the entry to the garden, which serves as an outdoor stage for even more sensory surprises and playful pleasures.

ROBERT MONDAVI WINERY

ROBERT MONDAVI WINERY
7801 Hwy. 29
Oakville, CA 94562
707-968-2001
888-766-6328
info@robertmondavi
winery.com
robertmondaviwinery.com

LOCATION: About 10 miles
north of the town of Napa.

APPELLATIONS: Oakville,
Napa Valley.

HOURS: 10 A.M.–5 P.M. daily.

TASTINGS: $20 for 4 wines
in main tasting room;
$45 for 4 wines or by the
glass in To Kalon Reserve
tasting room.

TOURS: Signature Tour
and Tasting, including
To Kalon Vineyard, by
reservation ($30); other
tours available seasonally.

THE WINES: Cabernet
Sauvignon, Chardonnay,
Fumé Blanc, I Block Fumé
Blanc, Merlot, Moscato
D'Oro, Pinot Noir, To
Kalon Cabernet Sauvignon.

SPECIALTIES: Cabernet
Sauvignon Reserve and
Fumé Blanc Reserve.

WINEMAKER:
Geneviève Janssens.

ANNUAL PRODUCTION:
250,000 cases.

OF SPECIAL NOTE: Private
cellar tasting and 4-course
wine-pairing dinner
available with advance
reservations. Large
shop with wine books
and Italian imports.
Summer Festival Concert
Series (July); Cabernet
Sauvignon Reserve Release
Party (September).

NEARBY ATTRACTIONS:
Culinary Institute of
America at Greystone
(cooking demonstrations);
Napa Valley Museum
(winemaking displays,
art exhibits).

Wineries come and wineries go in Napa Valley, but in this fast-paced, high-stakes world, few can challenge the lasting achievements of the Robert Mondavi Winery. Since its inception more than forty years ago, it has remained in the forefront of innovation, from the use of cold fermentation, stainless steel tanks, and small French oak barrels to the collaboration with NASA employing aerial imaging to reveal the health and vigor of grapevines.

Founder Robert Mondavi's cherished goal of producing wines on a par with the best in the world made his name virtually synonymous with California winemaking. That vision is being

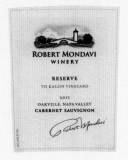

carried out today with ambitious programs such as the To Kalon Project. Named after the historic estate vineyard surrounding the winery, this extensive renovation led to the unveiling of the To Kalon Fermentation Cellar, which capitalizes on the natural flow of gravity to transport wine through the production system. Prized for their ability to enhance aromas, flavors, and complexity in red wines, the cellar's fifty-six French oak fermenting tanks were hand-crafted in Cognac by the renowned cooperage Taransaud. Coopers numbered each stave before disassembling the fermenters for shipping to Oakville, where the team reconstructed them in place at the winery.

Technological advances aside, the best reason for visiting Robert Mondavi Winery is something less tangible: an opportunity to experience the presentation of wine in the broader context of lifestyle. Educational tours and tastings, concerts, art exhibits, and the industry's first culinary programs are all part of the Mondavi legacy. One of the most popular offerings is the Signature Tour and Tasting, which follows the path of the grape from the vine through the cellar to the finished wine. The 550-acre vineyard was named To Kalon (Greek for "the beautiful") by Hamilton Walker Crabb, a wine-growing pioneer who established vineyards here in the late 1800s. It was this property that inspired Robert Mondavi to establish his winery on the site.

The winery's Spanish mission-style architecture, with its expansive archway and bell tower designed by Clifford May, pays homage to the Franciscan fathers who planted the first grapes in the region. Two long wings project from the open-air lobby to embrace a wide expanse of lawn framed by the Mayacamas Range on the western horizon. Typical of the winery's commitment to the arts, several sculptures by regional artist Beniamino Benvenuto Bufano (who, like Robert Mondavi's family, came from Italy) are displayed in the courtyard and elsewhere around the grounds. In addition, the winery features art exhibits that change every two months.

ROMBAUER VINEYARDS

The quarter-mile-long drive from the Silverado Trail leads to a winery ensconced in a forest of pine trees. On the far side of the low-slung building, a wide California ranch–style porch affords views that extend to the tree-covered ridge of the Mayacamas Range to the southeast. Without another structure in sight, the serene setting has the ambience of a fairy-tale kingdom secluded from the hustle and bustle of the valley floor. Directly below the winery, a gravel path winds down to a hill where roses are planted in the sun and azaleas thrive in the shade. Scattered about are a half-dozen metal sculptures of fantastical creatures such as a diminutive dinosaur and a life-size winged horse, all weathered to the point that they blend into the landscape.

The Rombauer family traces its heritage to another fertile wine area, the Rheingau region in Germany, where Koerner Rombauer's ancestors made wine. His great-aunt Irma Rombauer wrote the classic book *The Joy of Cooking*. The tradition of linking wine to food is carried on today, with every member of the family involved in the daily operation of the winery, from selecting grapes to marketing the final product.

Koerner Rombauer, a former commercial airline captain, and his late wife, Joan, met and married in Southern California, where both had grown up in an agricultural environment. Since they had always wanted their children to have rural childhood experiences similar to their own, they came to the Napa Valley in search of land. In 1972 they bought fifty acres and settled into a home just up the hill from where the winery sits today. Within a few years, they became partners in a nearby winery. Their hands-on involvement in the winery's operations whetted their appetite for a label of their own and for making handcrafted wines with the passion and commitment of the family tradition. Taking advantage of the topography, the Rombauers built their family winery into the side of the hill. Rombauer Vineyards was completed in 1982.

By the early 1990s, the Rombauers realized they had the perfect location for excavating wine storage caves. Completed in 1997, the double-horseshoe-shaped cellar extends for more than a mile into the hillside. When visitors enter the tasting room, they find a personalized space with an eclectic assortment of memorabilia from Koerner Rombauer's life. Guests may also get an occasional glimpse of another of Koerner's passions—one of the automobiles from his private collection of vintage cars.

ROMBAUER VINEYARDS
3522 Silverado Trail North
St. Helena, CA 94574
800-622-2206
707-963-5170
rombauer.com

OWNER:
Koerner Rombauer.

LOCATION: 1.5 miles north of Deer Park Rd.

APPELLATION: Napa Valley.

HOURS: 10 A.M.–5 P.M. daily.

TASTINGS: $20–$30, by appointment.

TOURS: Cave tours by appointment.

THE WINES: Cabernet Sauvignon, Chardonnay, Merlot, Zinfandel.

SPECIALTIES: Limited-production and single–vineyard Cabernet Sauvignon, Zinfandel, and Chardonnay; Best of the Cellar blend.

WINEMAKER: Richie Allen.

ANNUAL PRODUCTION: 130,000 cases.

OF SPECIAL NOTE: Copies of the latest edition of *The Joy of Cooking* and other cookbooks by Irma Rombauer are available in the tasting room. Zinfandel Port and Joy, a late-harvest Chardonnay, available only at winery.

NEARBY ATTRACTIONS: Culinary Institute of America at Greystone (cooking demonstrations); Bothe-Napa State Park (hiking, picnicking, horse-back riding, swimming Memorial Day–Labor Day); Robert Louis Stevenson Museum (author memorabilia).

RUTHERFORD HILL WINERY

RUTHERFORD HILL WINERY
200 Rutherford Hill Rd.
Rutherford, CA 94573
1-800-MERLOT1
707-963-1871
info@rutherfordhill.com
rutherfordhill.com

OWNERS: Terlato family.

LOCATION: About 2 miles south of St. Helena, just north of Rutherford Cross Rd. east of Silverado Trail.

APPELLATION: Rutherford.

HOURS: 10 A.M.–5 P.M. daily.

TASTINGS: $20–$30 for 5 wines.

TOURS: Cave tour and tasting. Reservations recommended.

THE WINES: Cabernet Franc, Cabernet Sauvignon, Chardonnay, Malbec, Merlot, Petit Verdot, Port, Rosé, Sauvignon Blanc.

SPECIALTIES: Merlot, Bordeaux blends.

WINEMAKER: Marisa Taylor.

ANNUAL PRODUCTION: 40,000 cases.

OF SPECIAL NOTE: Blend Your Own Merlot hands-on seminar. Bordeaux Meets Napa reserve tasting. Educational cave tours. (Reservations recommended for all special tastings and tours.) Picnic grounds with views. Winery is pet friendly. Reserve and limited-release wines available only in tasting room.

NEARBY ATTRACTIONS: Culinary Institute of America at Greystone (cooking demonstrations); Robert Louis Stevenson Museum (author memorabilia).

East of the Silverado Trail, a winding mountain road leads to one of Napa Valley's legendary wineries. Here, visitors will find Rutherford Hill Winery, tucked into a hillside and offering a stunning view of the valley. With its gambrel roof and rough-hewn redwood timbers, the winery resembles an antique barn. The impressive building is large enough to house both the winery and the inviting tasting room with its relaxed atmosphere. A pair of gigantic doors greets visitors as they approach the entrance. The winery is framed by expansive lawns and gardens, and a picnic area set in Napa Valley's oldest olive grove.

Rutherford Hill also possesses one of the largest wine-aging cave systems in North America. Begun in 1982 and completed by 1990, the caves are nearly a mile in length. They maintain a natural temperature of 59 degrees Fahrenheit and a relative humidity of 80 percent, conditions that provide the perfect environment and ecologically sensitive way to protect and age the wines. Entering the caves through large doors flanked by towering cypress, visitors immediately notice the heady perfumes of oak and aging Merlot and Cabernet.

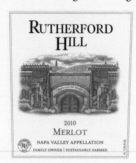

Rutherford Hill Winery was built in 1972 by Joseph Phelps, who soon went on to establish another winery in his own name. In 1976 Bill and Lila Jaeger bought the hilltop property, noting that the region's soils resembled those of Pomerol, a Bordeaux appellation famed for its outstanding Merlot-based wines. The local loam, or "Rutherford dust," a term coined in the late 1930s by famed Russian enologist André Tchelistcheff, is credited with imparting great depth and flavor to the area's plantings of Merlot and Cabernet Sauvignon.

In 1996 Anthony Terlato, a well-known figure in the American fine wine industry, acquired Rutherford Hill with the single-minded goal of producing the finest wines in the Rutherford appellation. Terlato had started his career in his father's Chicago retail wine shop in the 1950s and parlayed a modest business into a leading importer of fine wines. Shortly after purchasing Rutherford Hill, he built a state-of-the-art winery where the winemaker could separately vinify grapes coming from different vineyard lots and grown in many different and idiosyncratic soil types. This allowed the Terlatos and the winemaking team to focus on the specific vineyards producing the finest grapes, including nearly two hundred acres of estate vineyards that are now the foundation of Rutherford Hill wines. Today, Merlot makes up most of the winery's production, underscoring the enduring appeal of wines grown in the renowned Rutherford dust.

St. Clement Vineyards

Commanding a hilltop overlooking Napa Valley, the two-story Victorian home of St. Clement Vineyards offers a glimpse of gracious living from a bygone era. Its classic silhouette, complete with front gable, corbeled eaves, and Gothic tower, evokes a storybook destination untouched by time. Along one side, century-old olive trees grow, and on the other, live oaks and flower beds border a lush lawn. Worn stone steps lead up to the house and its wraparound porch, where a wooden swing invites a lazy sojourn. Above the front door, a stained glass transom reveals the home's original address.

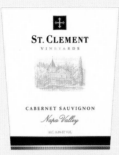

Built in 1878, the house was commissioned by a San Francisco glass importer who inaugurated its vinicultural tradition by making wine in the basement. The home sheltered several colorful owners, including a doctor and a pair of somewhat shady sisters, but by 1962 had fallen into disrepair. A real estate investor bought the manse and meticulously restored it, installing period crown molding, light fixtures, and doorknobs. He, too, made wine in the basement. Dr. William Casey, a local ophthalmologist, bought the five-acre property in 1975. He christened the estate St. Clement to honor family ties to Maryland, where a colonial landmark bears the saint's name. From that state's flag comes the cross visible on the label, carved into beams, and set into wrought iron fencing. Casey built a 4,000-square-foot winery behind the house in 1978, using locally quarried stone. With its weathered walls, false gable, and forestlike setting, the building looks like a century-old cellar. Inside, though, it is thoroughly modern, with a lofty platform that gives visitors a bird's-eye view of the work floor.

When Sapporo USA bought the property in 1988, the winery began producing a red wine called Oroppas (Sapporo spelled backward). That offering evolved into St. Clement's flagship wine: a magnificent Cabernet Sauvignon–based blend sourced from select Napa Valley vineyards in the Rutherford, Yountville, Diamond Mountain, Mt. Veeder, and Howell Mountain appellations.

Oroppas's and St. Clement's equally well-regarded single-vineyard Cabernet Sauvignons are the highlights of seated, appointment-only tastings that take place in the softly lit Winemaker's Vault, located behind the house in the stone winery. During these one-hour sessions amid oak aging barrels, a winery host shares the stories and history of the special hillside location while pouring the wines that are its legacy. Guests are invited to extend the pleasure of a stay here by bringing a picnic lunch and purchasing wine to enjoy at outdoor tables that are perfect for relaxing and admiring the views of Howell Mountain rising above the Napa Valley.

St. Clement Vineyards
2867 St. Helena Hwy.
North
St. Helena, CA 94574
866-877-5939
stclement.com

Location: 3 miles north of St. Helena on west side of St. Helena Hwy. North.

Appellation: Napa Valley.

Hours: By appointment (closed Tuesday and Wednesday).

Tastings: Seated tastings in Winemaker's Vault ($40), 11 A.M and 3 P.M. daily.

Tours: None.

The Wines: Cabernet Sauvignon, Chardonnay, Merlot, Sauvignon Blanc.

Specialty: Single-vineyard Cabernet Sauvignon.

Winemaker: Matt Johnson.

Annual Production: 20,000 cases.

Of Special Note: Century-old olive grove. Winery is pet friendly. Single-vineyard Cabernet Sauvignon available only in tasting room.

Nearby Attractions: Bothe-Napa State Park (hiking, picnicking, horseback riding, swimming Memorial Day–Labor Day); Bale Grist Mill State Historic Park (water-powered mill circa 1846); Culinary Institute of America (cooking demonstrations); Robert Louis Stevenson Museum (author memorabilia).

STAGS' LEAP WINERY

STAGS' LEAP WINERY
6150 Silverado Trail
Napa, CA 94558
800-395-2441
stagsleap.com

LOCATION: 7 miles north
of downtown Napa.

APPELLATION: Stags Leap
District.

HOURS: By appointment.

TASTINGS: $55 for 5 wines,
with tour, by appointment.

TOURS: 90-minute
historical tour included
with tasting. Reservations
required.

THE WINES: Cabernet
Sauvignon, Chardonnay,
Merlot, Petite Sirah, Rosé,
Viognier.

SPECIALTIES: Cabernet
Sauvignon, Ne Cede Malis
(old-vine Petite Sirah
blend).

WINEMAKER:
Christophe Paubert.

ANNUAL PRODUCTION:
100,000 cases.

OF SPECIAL NOTE: One
of Napa Valley's oldest
wineries. Historic Manor
House built in 1892.

NEARBY ATTRACTION:
Napa Valley Museum
(winemaking displays,
art exhibits).

To visit the Manor House at Stags' Leap Winery is to enter a world of Old California–style wealth, set amid 240 acres of pristine countryside. Like an elegant time capsule, the Romanesque mansion evokes the lavish dinners and lawn parties staged by its builder, San Francisco investor Horace B. Chase. Constructed in 1892 of locally quarried stone, the two-story house stands at the end of a driveway lined with fan palms and the low rock walls of terraced gardens. Mortared stone columns support the roof of a wraparound porch, and a castellated half-turret hosts a massive wisteria vine.

The Chases dubbed the estate Stag's Leap, a name attributed to a native Wappo legend of a stag leap-ing to elude hunters. The mountains behind the property then came to be called the Stags Leap Palisades. Producing wine to sell and share with friends, the Chases introduced the Stag's Leap Winery label in 1893. The Grange family bought the property in 1913 and turned it into a busy resort. The house sat empty from the early 1950s to 1970, when Carl Doumani spent four years restoring it. He revived the Stags' Leap Winery label, and in 1989 the Stags Leap District appellation (sans apostrophe) was recognized.

Visitors to the winery are greeted by friendly and informative staff who take them on a tour of the historic Manor House and the grounds. Paths winding among perennial gardens and vegetable beds offer enchanting views of the eighty-acre estate vineyard opposite the house. Inside the gracious Manor House, guests enjoy a seated tasting in the formal dining room, where soft light filters through Victorian leaded glass windows. Tastings are also held outdoors on a covered patio.

Bordeaux-born Christophe Paubert joined Stags' Leap Winery as winemaker in 2009, bringing an impressive background including serving as cellar master at the renowned Château d'Yquem in his native France and building a winery and overhauling a large vineyard in Chile. At Stags' Leap, he crafts balanced wines with the district's characteristic depth and soft tannins. His signature is the award-winning Leap Cabernet Sauvignon made from fruit sourced from a small, distinct vineyard block at the heart of the estate, whose well-drained volcanic soil is one factor that contributes to the reputation of the winery's Cabernet Sauvignon.

Reaching an elevation of 2,000 feet, the Stags Leap Palisades form a small, secluded valley. To find the winery, visitors take an unmarked Silverado Trail turnoff and travel a narrow country road between vineyards and walnut orchards. The effort is worth it—for Stags' Leap Winery glimmers with the magic of that mighty buck.

STERLING VINEYARDS

An eye-catching complex of bright white walls and curved bell towers, Sterling Vineyards crowns a forested volcanic knoll three hundred feet above the Napa Valley floor. The winery, which from a distance could double as a hilltop Greek island monastery, commands sweeping views of the geometric vineyards and foothills below. To reach it, visitors leave their cars in the parking lot and board an aerial tramway—the only one of its kind in the valley—for a solar-powered glide over a glistening pond, pines, and live oaks to a walkway among the treetops.

A self-guided tour encourages visitors to explore the stately facility at their own pace, while strategically stationed hosts pour wine samples along the way. Illustrated signboards describe points of interest, and motion-activated flat-screen televisions display videos of winemaking activity. Bells from a former tenth-century London church chime on the quarter hour, their rich tones ringing across exterior foot-paths that afford elevated views of the crush pad and fermentation area. Inside the winery, visitors may observe employees at work among stainless steel and redwood tanks, and peek at some of the winery's 25,000 barrels as they impart delicate flavors to the wine aging within. On the South View Terrace, redwood planters brim with lavender and ornamental grasses, and two sixty-foot-tall Italian cypresses frame the scene to the south. Here, guests sip wine as they take in the panoramic vistas of vineyards, neighboring estates, and parts of the Mayacamas Range on the Sonoma-Napa border, where Mount St. Helena rises above the neighboring peaks to an elevation of 4,343 feet.

Englishman Peter Newton, founder of Sterling Paper International, started the winery in 1964, when he bought a fifty-acre pasture just north of the town of Calistoga. He surprised local vintners by planting Merlot—at the time considered a minor blending grape—along with Chardonnay, Cabernet Sauvignon, and Sauvignon Blanc. Five years later, Newton bottled his first wines, which included California's earliest vintage-dated Merlot. In the early 1980s, the winery purchased one thousand vineyard acres on fourteen different Napa Valley ranches, giving the winemaker a broad spectrum of fruit to work with, as well as control over the farming of the grapes. The winery continues to source fruit from these and two hundred additional acres of select Napa Valley vineyards in various appellations such as Calistoga, St. Helena, Rutherford, and Carneros.

Sterling Vineyards built a reserve wine production facility on the valley floor in 2002, but visitors should make touring the hilltop winery their top priority, as it is one of the most memorable experiences in the Napa Valley.

STERLING VINEYARDS
1111 Dunaweal Ln.
Calistoga, CA 94515
707-942-3300
800-726-6136
info@sterlingvineyards.com
sterlingvineyards.com

OWNER: Diageo Chateau and Estate Wines.

LOCATION: 1 mile southeast of Calistoga.

APPELLATION: Calistoga.

HOURS: 10:30 A.M.–5 P.M. Monday–Friday; 10 A.M.–5 P.M. Saturday–Sunday. Closed major holidays.

TASTINGS: $29 admission for aerial tram ride, self-guided tour, 5 wine tastes, and souvenir glass. For additional tastings of reserve and limited-release wines, visit the website.

TOURS: Self-guided.

THE WINES: Cabernet Franc, Cabernet Sauvignon, Chardonnay, Malvasia Bianca, Merlot, Muscat Canelli, Petite Sirah, Pinot Gris, Pinot Noir, Sangiovese, Sauvignon Blanc, Syrah, Viognier, Zinfandel.

SPECIALTIES: Merlot, Cabernet Sauvignon, Platinum (Bordeaux blend).

WINEMAKER: Harry Hansen.

ANNUAL PRODUCTION: Unavailable.

OF SPECIAL NOTE: Display of Ansel Adams photographs and wine-related art.

NEARBY ATTRACTIONS: Robert Louis Stevenson Museum (author memorabilia); Napa Valley Museum (winemaking displays, art exhibits).

SULLIVAN VINEYARDS

SULLIVAN VINEYARDS
1090 Galleron Rd.
Rutherford, CA 94573
707-963-9646
877-244-7337
info@sullivanwine.com
sullivanwine.com

OWNERS: Sullivan family.

LOCATION: 3.5 miles southeast of downtown St. Helena.

APPELLATION: Rutherford.

HOURS: 10:30 A.M.–4 P.M. daily in summer; 11 A.M.–4 P.M. daily in winter.

TASTINGS: $25 for 4 current release wines; $50 for 4 library reserve wines; $75 for VIP food-and-wine pairing. By appointment.

TOURS: None.

THE WINES: Cabernet Sauvignon, Chardonnay, Merlot, Sauvignon Blanc.

SPECIALTIES: Small-lot estate Cabernet Sauvignon and Merlot, Coeur de Vigne (Bordeaux blend).

WINEMAKERS: Scott McLeod, consulting winemaker; Jeff Cole, assistant winemaker.

ANNUAL PRODUCTION: 5,000 cases.

OF SPECIAL NOTE: Seated indoor and outdoor tastings. Tree-shaded pond. Original paintings by Sullivan family member in tasting room. Most wines from estate-grown fruit. Classic cars on display. All wines available only at winery.

NEARBY ATTRACTIONS: Culinary Institute of America at Greystone (cooking demonstrations); Bale Grist Mill State Historic Park (water-powered mill circa 1846); Robert Louis Stevenson Museum (author memorabilia).

In 1972 Jim and Joanna Sullivan transplanted their family from Los Angeles to Rutherford so that Jim, a graphic designer for Hollywood companies, could pursue his vision of producing Cabernet Sauvignon wines. Jim reflected years later that he decided early on to focus on "the king of grapes" because it makes "serious," complex wines. The family acquired the current twenty-six-acre Sullivan Vineyards site in 1978, roughing it for several years in a trailer with a screened porch before moving into the redwood-clad California Arts and Crafts–style home that still anchors the estate.

John Marsh Davis, whose previous projects include the Joseph Phelps Vineyards winery, designed the house and a companion winery. For financial reasons, the Sullivans delayed implementing some of Davis's plan. Only in

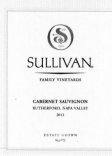

2014 was the wraparound redwood deck he envisioned finally completed. Davis was known for cleverly positioning buildings to make the most of their landscapes. It's worth walking around the house to its eastern side to appreciate how this valley-floor structure appears to hover over the vineyards, as though suspended on a hillside above them.

Those vineyards nurture mostly Cabernet Sauvignon and Merlot grapes used to make small-lot wines. As the original winemaker, Jim Sullivan favored fruit-forward yet structured wines meant to age well. The current winemaking team, led by Scott McLeod, is refining Jim's style, focusing on wines that express the soil and sunny climate of this terrain near the Rutherford appellation's northern border. During his eighteen-year tenure at nearby Rubicon Estate (now Inglenook), McLeod was named Winemaker of the Year by *Wine Enthusiast* magazine and won numerous awards for the flagship Rubicon wine.

Tastings at Sullivan are seated, leisurely affairs conducted in a light-filled salon inside the winery or on a courtyard between it and the Sullivan home. The living-room-like salon, renovated in 2014, showcases the paintings of Jim and Joanna's daughter, Kelleen Sullivan Finn, who provides a new label for each vintage of the Coeur de Vigne (Heart of the Vineyard) Bordeaux-style blend. A huge sycamore tree and saffron-colored umbrellas shade the courtyard, where finches warble a tuneful soundtrack from their perches above classic cars from the family collection.

The winery's personable staffers are equally comfortable discussing the intricacies of the wines or relating Sullivan family anecdotes. Jim's sons Ross and Sean, who are still involved with the business, occasionally drop by and share firsthand memories. Recent years have seen family wineries transformed into party palaces, but the second Sullivan generation has chosen to retain the feel of a stylish family home, making a visit here a rare and serene pleasure.

SWANSON VINEYARDS

The gates at Swanson Vineyards swing open as if admitting entry to a private estate. Indeed, the winery's shaded courtyard, terra-cotta-colored walls, and blue shutters give it the look of a villa in rural Provence. Owners Clarke and Elizabeth Swanson enhanced the French theme in 2000, when they built the tasting room and offered the region's first seated, appointment-only tastings. Elizabeth, a New Orleans native, partnered with noted Bay Area figurative artist Ira Yeager and renowned interior designer Thomas Britt to create a space with the lush textures and features of a bygone era. Called the Swanson Salon, the regal tasting room evokes eighteenth-century Paris so effectively that it feels as if a lively literary gathering might convene at any moment. Displayed on the bright watermelon-hued walls are Yeager's fanciful paintings of eighteenth-century wine vendors. A French stone fireplace provides winter warmth, and a seventeenth-century portal holding a full-length mirror gives the impression of lavish rooms beyond.

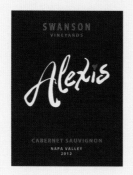

The salonnière greets guests with a glass of wine and seats them around an octagonal Moroccan table inlaid with agates. Limited to eight people, the tastings are like private dinner parties animated by spirited conversation. The intimate setting invites a leisurely enjoyment of the wines, which are accompanied by sumptuous small bites, such as aged cheese, potato chips topped with crème fraîche and caviar, and a signature chocolate bonbon. To offer a more casual experience, the Swansons opened the Sip Shoppe next door in 2010. Here visitors sample wines amid the festive atmosphere of a circus tent stocked with antiques and eclectic gift items. Red-and-white-striped canvas covers the walls of what staffers hail as a candy store for adults.

The Swansons founded the winery in 1985, the same year they planted wine grapes on a hundred-acre parcel in the Oakville appellation. Although the region was renowned for its Cabernet Sauvignon, the Swansons took the advice of noted winemaker André Tchelistcheff and planted Merlot instead. Agricultural pursuits came naturally to Clarke, whose grandfather operated poultry farms and creameries. Clarke, who graduated from Stanford University in 1961, went on to succeed in banking and as an entrepreneur specializing in radio, cable television, and community newspapers. His entry to the wine business was spurred at his twenty-fifth college reunion, when Bob Travers, a former fraternity brother and owner of Mayacamas Vineyards, convinced him to purchase property in Oakville. Among the first in Napa Valley to bottle Merlot as a stand-alone wine, the family-owned winery ranks as one of the region's premier producers of the variety.

SWANSON VINEYARDS
1271 Manley Ln.
Rutherford, CA 94573
707-754-4018
salon@swansonvineyards.com
swansonvineyards.com

OWNER: W. Clarke Swanson.

LOCATION: 200 yards west of Hwy. 29.

APPELLATIONS: Oakville, Napa Valley.

HOURS: 11 A.M., 1:30 P.M., and 4 P.M. Wednesday–Monday in Salon. 11 A.M.–4 P.M. Thursday–Monday in Sip Shoppe. Both by appointment.

TASTINGS: $25 in Sip Shoppe; $65 in Salon.

TOURS: None.

THE WINES: Cabernet Sauvignon, Chardonnay, Merlot, Petite Sirah, Pinot Grigio, Sangiovese, Sauvignon Blanc, sweet wines, Viognier.

SPECIALTIES: Small-batch wines.

WINEMAKER: Chris Phelps.

ANNUAL PRODUCTION: 20,000 cases.

OF SPECIAL NOTE: Clarke's Bark and Alexis bonbons and candy bar, made in collaboration with Vosges, are sold at the winery.

NEARBY ATTRACTIONS: Robert Louis Stevenson Museum (author memorabilia); Napa Valley Museum (winemaking displays, art exhibits); Culinary Institute of America at Greystone (cooking demonstrations).

WHITEHALL LANE WINERY

WHITEHALL LANE WINERY
1563 Hwy. 29
St. Helena, CA 94574
800-963-9454
greatwine@
whitehalllane.com
whitehalllane.com

OWNER:
Thomas Leonardini Sr.

LOCATION: 2 miles south
of St. Helena.

APPELLATION: Rutherford.

HOURS: 10 A.M.–5:30 P.M.
daily.

TASTINGS: $15 for current
releases; price varies for
reserve selections. No
reservations required.
Seated tastings by
appointment.

TOURS: By appointment.

THE WINES: Cabernet
Sauvignon, Chardonnay,
dessert wine, Merlot, Pinot
Noir, Sauvignon Blanc.

SPECIALTIES: Reserve
Cabernet Sauvignon,
Leonardini Vineyard
Cabernet Sauvignon,
Millennium MM Vineyard
Cabernet Sauvignon.

WINEMAKER: Dean Sylvester.

ANNUAL PRODUCTION:
45,000 cases.

OF SPECIAL NOTE: Limited-
production Leonardini
Family Selection wines
available only at the winery.

NEARBY ATTRACTIONS:
Bothe-Napa State Park
(hiking, picnicking,
horseback riding, swimming
Memorial Day–Labor
Day); Culinary Institute
of America at Greystone
(cooking demonstrations);
Robert Louis Stevenson
Museum (author
memorabilia); Napa Valley
Museum (winemaking
displays, art exhibits).

Ocher and lavender, the colors of a California sunset, soften the geometric lines of Whitehall Lane, an angular, contemporary structure that stands in contrast to the pastoral setting of the vineyard. As if to telegraph the business at hand, the building's large windows have been cut in the shape of wine goblets. In front of the winery, a single row of square pillars runs alongside a walkway, each pillar supporting a vine that has entwined itself in the overhanging pergola.

Glass doors open into a tasting room with a white beamed ceiling, cream walls with black-and-white photos of the vineyard, black counters, and concrete bar tops. The handsome interior befits an estate where the first grapevines were planted in 1880. Even then, Napa Valley settlers were drawn to Rutherford's deep, loamy soils and sunny climate. A vestige of those days, a barn built for equipment storage, is still in use today.

In 1979 two brothers bought the twenty-six-acre vineyard and founded the winery they named after the road that runs along the south border of the property. They produced Merlot and Cabernet Sauvignon before selling the property nine years later. The Leonardini family of San Francisco took over the Whitehall Lane Estate in 1993. Tom Leonardini, already a wine aficionado, had been looking for property to purchase. He was aware of the winery's premium vineyard sources and some of its outstanding wines. Moreover, unlike his previous enterprises, the winery presented an opportunity to create a business that could involve his entire family.

Leonardini updated the winemaking and instituted a new barrel-aging program. He also replanted the estate vineyard in Merlot and Sauvignon Blanc and began acquiring additional grape sources. Whitehall Lane now owns six Napa Valley vineyards, a total of 150 acres on the valley floor: the Estate Vineyard, the Millennium MM Vineyard, the Bommarito Vineyard, the Leonardini Vineyard, the Fawn Park Vineyard, and the Oak Glen Vineyard. The various wines produced from these vineyards were rated among the top five in the world on three occasions by *Wine Spectator* magazine.

Whitehall Lane's new building contains a barrel room and a crush pad, as well as a second-floor VIP tasting room. The goal of the facility is not to increase overall production, but to focus on small lots of Cabernet Sauvignon produced from the St. Helena and Rutherford vineyards. As the winery approaches its thirty-sixth anniversary, the Leonardinis have many reasons to celebrate the success of their family business.

ZD WINES

Driving along the Silverado Trail through the heart of Napa Valley, travelers are sure to notice ZD Wines. A two-ton boulder, from one of ZD's mountain vineyards, is adorned with the winery's striking gold logo, beckoning all to visit. A walkway lined with California native plants and grasses leads to the winery entrance. Inside the tasting room, a five-foot soil monolith showcases the foundation of another vineyard. Visitors find a cool respite on a hot summer day or a cozy place to linger in front of a fireplace in winter. Behind the tasting bar, large windows look into the ZD cellar, offering a glimpse of where the Chardonnay, Pinot Noir, and Cabernet Sauvignon they are sipping is crafted.

It has been said that winemaking isn't rocket science, but in fact, founding partner Norman deLeuze had been designing liquid  rocket engines for Aerojet-General in Sacramento when he met his partner Gino Zepponi. They decided to collaborate on producing classic Pinot Noir and Chardonnay and needed a name for their new enterprise. The aeronautical industry had a quality-control program with the initials ZD, referring to Zero Defects. This matched the partners' initials and created a new association for the letters ZD. In 1969 the winery purchased Pinot Noir grapes from the Winery Lake Vineyard in Carneros in southern Sonoma and produced its first wine, which was also the first wine ever labeled with the Carneros appellation. Soon after, the winery started making Chardonnay, ZD's flagship wine today.

Norman deLeuze turned to winemaking full-time, while his wife, Rosa Lee, handled sales and marketing. They purchased six acres, built their own winery, and planted Cabernet Sauvignon in Rutherford in 1979. Four years later, son Robert deLeuze was named winemaker. He had been working in ZD's cellars since he was twelve. In 2001 Robert passed the winemaking reins to Chris Pisani, who had worked closely with Robert for five years, building his appreciation and understanding of the family's consistent winemaking style.

Owned and operated by the deLeuzes for more than four decades, ZD Wines is a testament to the traditions, heritage, and passion of a true family business. Their success in crafting world-class wine has made them one of Napa Valley's iconic families. Founders Norman and Rosa Lee's two sons are currently at the helm of the winery: Robert deLeuze as CEO and wine master and Brett deLeuze as president. Grandchildren Brandon and Jill deLeuze bring in the family's third generation, Brandon as associate winemaker and Jill as California sales manager.

ZD WINES
8383 Silverado Trail
Napa, CA 94558
800-487-7757
zdwines.com

OWNERS: deLeuze family.

LOCATION: About 2.5 miles south of Zinfandel Ln.

APPELLATION: Rutherford.

HOURS: 10 A.M.–4:30 P.M. daily.

TASTINGS: $15 for 3 or 4 current releases; $30 for 2 or 3 reserve or library wines.

TOURS: By appointment. Cellar Tour ($50), Eco Tour ($60), Vineyard View ($95).

THE WINES: Cabernet Sauvignon, Chardonnay, Pinot Noir.

SPECIALTY: Abacus (solera-style blend of ZD Reserve Cabernet Sauvignon).

WINEMAKERS: Robert deLeuze, wine master; Chris Pisani, winemaker; Brandon deLeuze, associate winemaker.

ANNUAL PRODUCTION: 30,000 cases.

OF SPECIAL NOTE: Abacus tasting—comprehensive tour of cellar and tasting of reserve wines with a focus on Abacus, $700 for up to 6 guests.

NEARBY ATTRACTIONS: Bothe-Napa State Park (hiking, picnicking, horseback riding, swimming Memorial Day–Labor Day); Robert Louis Stevenson Museum (author memorabilia).

SONOMA

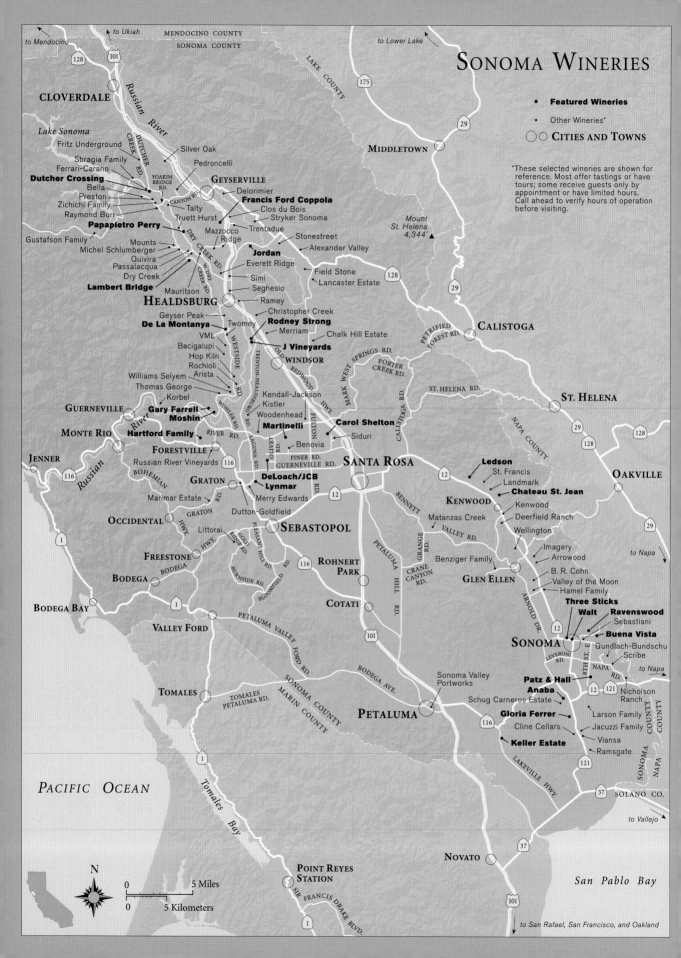

SONOMA WINERIES

- • **Featured Wineries**
- • Other Wineries*
- ◯ ◯ CITIES AND TOWNS

*These selected wineries are shown for reference. Most offer tastings or have tours; some receive guests only by appointment or have limited hours. Call ahead to verify hours of operation before visiting.

to Mendocino
to Ukiah
MENDOCINO COUNTY
SONOMA COUNTY
to Lower Lake

128
101
175
29

CLOVERDALE

Russian River
Lake Sonoma

Fritz Underground
Silver Oak
Sbragia Family
Pedroncelli
Ferrari-Carano
Dutcher Crossing
Bella
Preston
Zichichi Family
Raymond Burr
Papapietro Perry
Gustafson Family

YOAKIM BRIDGE RD.
DUTCHER CREEK RD.
CANYON RD.
GEYSERVILLE
Delorimier
Francis Ford Coppola
Talty
Clos du Bois
Truett Hurst
Stryker Sonoma
Mazzocco
Trentadue
Ridge

Mount St. Helena 4,344'

29

CALISTOGA

Stonestreet
Alexander Valley

Mounts
Michel Schlumberger
Quivira
Passalacqua
Dry Creek
Lambert Bridge
Mauritson

Jordan
Everett Ridge
Simi
Seghesio
Ramey
Field Stone
Lancaster Estate

128

DRY CREEK RD.
W. DRY CREEK RD.

29

HEALDSBURG

Geyser Peak
De La Montanya
Twomey
Christopher Creek
Rodney Strong
Merriam
Chalk Hill Estate

PETRIFIED FOREST RD.

ST. HELENA

VML
Bacigalupi
Hop Kiln
Rochioli
Arista
Williams Selyem
Thomas George
Korbel

J Vineyards
WINDSOR

WESTSIDE RD.
TRENTON-HEALDSBURG
OLD REDWOOD HWY.

MARK WEST SPRINGS RD.
PORTER CREEK RD.
ST. HELENA RD.
CALISTOGA RD.

NAPA COUNTY

29
128
128

OAKVILLE

GUERNEVILLE
Gary Farrell
Moshin
Hartford Family

Russian River

Kendall-Jackson
Kistler
Woodenhead
Martinelli
Benovia
Carol Shelton
Siduri

FULTON RD.
OLIVET RD.

Ledson
St. Francis
Landmark
Chateau St. Jean
Kenwood
Deerfield Ranch
Wellington

29

to Napa

MONTE RIO

FORESTVILLE
Russian River Vineyards

WOHLER RD.
RIVER RD.
LAGUNA RD.
PINER RD.
GUERNEVILLE RD.

SANTA ROSA

12

KENWOOD
Matanzas Creek

VALLEY RD.

Imagery
Arrowood
B. R. Cohn
Valley of the Moon
Hamel Family

JENNER

116

GRATON
Marimar Estate

GRATON HWY.
Littorai
116

DeLoach/JCB
Lynmar
Merry Edwards
Dutton-Goldfield

12

BENNETT

Benziger Family

GLEN ELLEN

ARNOLD DR.

Three Sticks
Walt
Ravenswood
Sebastiani

1

OCCIDENTAL

BOHEMIAN HWY.
PLEASANT HILL RD.
GOLD RIDGE RD.

SEBASTOPOL

PETALUMA HILL RD.
GRANGE RD.
CRANE CANYON RD.

12

Buena Vista
SONOMA
Gundlach-Bundschu
Scribe

FREESTONE

BODEGA HWY.
BURNSIDE RD.
BLOOMFIELD RD.

116
ROHNERT PARK

LEVERONI RD.
8TH ST. E.
NAPA RD.

to Napa

BODEGA

COTATI

Patz & Hall
Anaba
Schug Carneros Estate

12
121
Nicholson Ranch

BODEGA BAY

1

VALLEY FORD

101

Gloria Ferrer
Cline Cellars

Larson Family
Jacuzzi Family
Viansa
Ramsgate

116

Keller Estate

PETALUMA VALLEY FORD RD.

BODEGA AVE.

Sonoma Valley Portworks

TOMALES

TOMALES PETALUMA RD.
SONOMA COUNTY
MARIN COUNTY

PETALUMA

121

SONOMA COUNTY
NAPA COUNTY

37
SOLANO CO.

1

to Vallejo

PACIFIC OCEAN

Tomales Bay

37

N

0 — 5 Miles
0 — 5 Kilometers

POINT REYES STATION

SIR FRANCIS DRAKE BLVD.

1

NOVATO

101

San Pablo Bay

to San Rafael, San Francisco, and Oakland

Sonoma boasts the greatest geographical diversity in California wine country. From the Pacific Coast to the inland valleys, to the Mayacamas Range that defines the eastern border with Napa County, the countryside is crisscrossed by dozens of rural roads, making it an ideal destination for casual exploration.

Most of the county's oldest wineries can be found in the historic town of Sonoma. Facing the extensively landscaped eight-acre central plaza are nineteenth-century adobe and false-front buildings that now  house upscale shops, restaurants, and inns, as well as historic sites.

In the northern part of the county, the city of Healdsburg has recently evolved from a quiet backwater into the hottest destination in Sonoma County. It sits at the hub of three major grape-growing regions—Russian River Valley, Alexander Valley, and Dry Creek Valley—all within a ten-minute drive of the vibrant town plaza.

North of Santa Rosa, the Russian River Valley extends from the Healdsburg area almost all the way to the ocean, where the Sonoma Coast has become one of the most sought-after wine appellations. In addition to the colorful villages clustered along the coastal routes, the region offers boating, swimming, and fishing opportunities and the shade of giant redwoods that soar above the Russian River's banks.

ANABA WINES

Tasters step into history when they visit the Anaba Wines tasting room in a farmhouse built a century ago. A simple structure, it features the high-pitched roof, front gable, and full-width porch typical of California's early rural construction. Fronted by two thirty-foot-tall Canary Island date palms—survivors of the original landscaping—it radiates a powerful sense of place. Nearby, a wind turbine cuts a striking figure against a backdrop of sky and the chaparral-streaked foothills of the Sonoma Mountains. Towering forty-five feet tall, it offers a clue to the meaning of the winery's intriguing name. Anaba (pronounced "anna-bah") derives from the word *anabatic,* which means "moving upward" and perfectly describes the Carneros appellation's climate-defining winds.

When cool breezes off San Pablo Bay, located ten miles south, meet warm mountain slopes inland, they drift upward. The swirling winds drive away fog in the morning and cool the vineyards in the afternoon, which enhances the ripening process. They also spin the turbine's blades, generating clean power for the winery. Owners John and Kathleen Sweazey have taken further steps to run a green operation by sustainably farming the estate vineyards beside the farmhouse. They source additional fruit from vineyards throughout Sonoma County. In each location they meticulously farm their designated blocks. As a result, Anaba boasts an eclectic array of exquisite, small-lot Burgundian and Rhône-style wines. For fans of dessert wines, there are white and red Port-style wines, fortified with spirits distilled from estate-grown grapes.

A Chicago native, John discovered wine as a student at Stanford, where he spent weekends exploring Napa and Sonoma counties. After graduating with an economics degree in 1967, he spent nine months in Europe and developed an affinity for the wines of France's Rhône and Burgundy regions. Back in San Francisco, he built a successful real estate finance company and even did a little home winemaking. In 2006 John and Kathleen bought the Carneros property, which included eight acres of vineyards, most of which they replanted to Chardonnay and aromatic whites. Two years later, the couple introduced the Anaba label. They lovingly restored the farmhouse, fashioning the front living area into a tasting room, and opened to the public in 2009.

The room's vintage brick fireplace, open-beam ceiling, and ceramic pitcher full of fresh flowers reinforce the impression of a comfortable country home. Double french doors open onto a spacious redwood deck, where staff often pour seated tastings. The sheltered deck overlooks a lawn bordered by tidy beds of mixed roses, lavender, and ornamental grasses. Beyond the beds grow Chardonnay vines, their leaves gently rustling in the region's signature anabatic breezes.

ANABA WINES
60 Bonneau Rd.
Sonoma, CA 95476
877-990-4188
inquiry@anabawines.com
anabawines.com

OWNERS: John and Kathleen Sweazey.

LOCATION: 4 miles south of the town of Sonoma at the intersection of Hwy. 121 and 116.

APPELLATION: Los Carneros.

HOURS: 10:30 A.M.–5:30 P.M. daily.

TASTINGS: $10 for 6 current release wines.

TOURS: By appointment.

THE WINES: Chardonnay, Grenache, Mourvèdre, Petite Sirah, Pinot Noir, Port, Rosé, Syrah, Viognier.

SPECIALTIES: Vineyard-designated Chardonnay and Pinot Noir, Rhône-style blends.

WINEMAKERS: Ross Cobb, Katy Wilson.

ANNUAL PRODUCTION: 7,500 cases.

OF SPECIAL NOTE: Tasting room located in a 100-year-old farmhouse. Tasting on a deck overlooking the vineyard. Wine available for purchase by the glass. Port-style wines, late-harvest Viognier, and most vineyard-designated wines available only in tasting room.

NEARBY ATTRACTIONS: Mission San Francisco Solano, Lachryma Montis (Mariano Vallejo's estate), and other historic buildings in downtown Sonoma; Sonoma Raceway (NASCAR and other events); biplane flights; Cornerstone Sonoma (garden installations by landscape architects).

BUENA VISTA WINERY

BUENA VISTA WINERY
18000 Old Winery Rd.
Sonoma, CA 95476
800-926-1266
tastingroom@
buenavistawinery.com
buenavistawinery.com

OWNER: Boisset Collection.

LOCATION: 2.3 miles east of historic Sonoma Plaza.

APPELLATIONS: Los Carneros, Sonoma Valley, Sonoma Coast, Alexander Valley.

HOURS: 10 A.M.–5 P.M. daily.

TASTINGS: $15 for 5 wines; $20 for 4 reserve wines.

TOURS: Hour-long tour of historic caves with Barrel Tour and Tasting ($35), 11 A.M. and 2 P.M. by appointment.

THE WINES: Carignane, Charbono, Chardonnay, French Colombard, Grenache, Merlot, Pinot Gris, Pinot Meunier, Pinot Noir, Pinot Noir Rosé, Sauvignon Blanc, Sparkling Brut, Valdique, Zinfandel.

SPECIALTIES: Private Reserve Pinot Noir, Chardonnay, Zinfandel; unique historic varietals.

WINEMAKER: Brian Maloney; consulting winemaker: David Ramey.

ANNUAL PRODUCTION: 70,000 cases.

OF SPECIAL NOTE: Picnic hampers, cheese, crackers, and wines by the glass or by the bottle for purchase. Tree-shaded picnic area and terraces. Winery is family friendly and pet friendly. Gift shop. Shakespeare festival in August. Museum with historic wine tools. Private Reserve, Vinicultural Society, and Sparkling Brut wines available only in the tasting room.

NEARBY ATTRACTIONS: Historic buildings in downtown Sonoma.

When Hungarian Count Agoston Haraszthy arrived in California in the 1840s, other pioneers and immigrants were beginning to pour in, lured by the prospect of gold and other opportunities. In 1856 the count, a flamboyant vinicultural pioneer, acquired eight-hundred-acre Buena Vista Ranch in Sonoma and introduced grapevines imported from Europe. Prior to this, the only wine grapes in Sonoma were Mission grapes planted and tended by the Franciscan friars who founded a mission on what is now Sonoma Plaza. In 1857 Haraszthy established Buena Vista Winery, the first premium winery in the state. He also built a massive stone winery with the nation's first gravity-flow facilities and excavated California's first wine caves.

Fast-forward to harvest 2012 — when Buena Vista Winery emerged from an extensive renovation of the original winery, caves, and grounds. Boisset Collection purchased Buena Vista in 2011. Jean-Charles Boisset, president of the family business, had visited Buena Vista on his first trip to California when he was eleven years old. The deep sense of history and the verdant setting made an indelible impression. Later, after settling in Napa, he pounced on the opportunity to acquire the historic winery. Boisset, whose passion for California wines and pioneering spirit are often compared with Count Haraszthy's, immediately launched plans to restore the estate to its former glory while adding twenty-first-century equipment for crafting premium wines. The 2012 harvest marked the first vintage to be made in the historic cellars in decades. Winemakers Brian Maloney and David Ramey oversee wine production, which includes five collections.

A visit to Buena Vista is a rare chance to experience firsthand California's rich winemaking heritage and Buena Vista's storied past. The fully restored buildings and grounds include cobblestone terraces, a vortex fountain, a demonstration vineyard with examples of original vines the count brought from Europe, and a heritage garden with fruits and vegetables grown in the Americas. Regular flights are poured in the two-story historic stone press house. Guides dressed as historic Buena Vista characters are on hand to tell tales of the winery's early days. The barrel tasting and tour, the private reserve tasting, tastings in the elegant Bubble Room, and a ninety-minute Be the Count — Winemaker for a Day blending session take place in the historic Champagne Cellars.

Guests are encouraged to picnic on the grounds, visit the museum displaying antique wine tools, and browse the second floor of the historic Press House, filled with exhibits about Count Haraszthy and Buena Vista Winery's 150-year-old tale.

CAROL SHELTON WINES

The last place most people would think to look for a well-respected winery's tasting room is in an anonymous complex of cookie-cutter office and warehouse buildings in an industrial district in Santa Rosa. When visitors enter the Carol Shelton Wines tasting room, however, the urban-industrial vibe disappears. The cheery interior of the intimate space feels like a parlor in a casual family home. Custom-designed paintings decorate the walls, along with hundreds of ribbons and numerous news articles—testaments to Carol Shelton's stellar reputation for winemaking.

Shelton's path toward an eventual interest in wine began when she was just six years old, and her mother developed an "identify the scent" game using everyday herbs and spices. Shelton quickly exhibited a keen sense of smell and proved adept at figuring out new scents as the game evolved. She later entered U.C. Davis with a penchant for poetry but shifted direction after her first visit to a wine cellar. The alluring aroma of wine aging in oak barrels led Shelton to major in enology. After graduation, she worked at renowned cellars and alongside industry giants, including André Tchelistcheff, Zelma Long at Robert Mondavi, and Peter Lehmann in Australia's Barossa Valley. She also worked for nearly twenty years at Windsor Vineyards in Sonoma County, where she bottled forty-five different wines each year. Over time, she developed a particular passion for Zinfandel because she relished the challenge of taking the user-friendly, fruit-forward grape to make wines with balanced alcohol, sugar, and oak influences.

In 2000 Shelton and her husband, Mitch Mackenzie, a former HP software engineer, launched their own brand—Carol Shelton Wines—which focuses on her beloved Zinfandels. She carefully selects trusted vineyards in appellations throughout California that have stellar fruit reflecting the *terroir* of the region. Each Zinfandel bears a whimsical name that echoes her fondness for words and wine: Wild Thing, made with wild yeasts; Karma Zin, a nod to the good fortune that led Shelton to a field blend vineyard with exceptional grapes; Monga Zin, a play on the wine's "humongous" flavor, produced from fruit from the Cucamonga Valley in Southern California; and Rocky Reserve, which uses grapes from the Rockpile appellation. In addition to Zinfandels, Shelton makes Coquille Blanc (a white Rhône blend), a Pinot Noir, two Petite Sirahs, and a dry Rosé.

Guests taste Shelton's latest vintages at a portable teak bar in a space filled with eclectic furnishings, wine barrels, and a small piano. They are welcome to request a five-minute tour of the on-site winemaking facility and barrel room and to learn more about her well-honed olfactory senses and the years of expertise that have gone into crafting her much-lauded wines.

CAROL SHELTON WINES
3354-B Coffey Ln.
Santa Rosa, CA 95403
707-575-3441
wines@carolshelton.com
carolshelton.com

OWNERS: Carol Shelton and Mitch Mackenzie.

LOCATION: 2.5 miles west of U.S. 101 in Pine Creek Business Park, on east side of Coffey Ln., north of Piner Rd.

APPELLATIONS: Rockpile, Russian River Valley, Sonoma Coast, Los Carneros, Paso Robles, Cucamonga Valley.

HOURS: 11 A.M.–4 P.M. daily.

TASTINGS: Complimentary for 6 or 7 wines; $5 per person for group of 7 or more tasters.

TOURS: Complimentary for winemaking facility, subject to staff availability.

THE WINES: Cabernet Sauvignon, Carignane, Coquille Blanc (white Rhône blend), dry Rosé, Late Harvest Zinfandel, Petite Sirah, Pinot Noir, Zinfandel.

SPECIALTY: Zinfandel.

WINEMAKER: Carol Shelton.

ANNUAL PRODUCTION: 15,000 cases.

OF SPECIAL NOTE: Winery is pet friendly. Annual events include March Barrel Tasting weekends and summer luau (last Saturday in July). Pinot Noir, Petite Sirah, Cabernet Sauvignon, and some reserve and library Zinfandel wines available only in tasting room.

NEARBY ATTRACTIONS: Charles M. Schulz Museum (exhibits on *Peanuts* creator and other cartoonists); Snoopy's Home Ice (ice-skating arena); Luther Burbank Garden and Home (tours of famed horticulturalist's property).

CHATEAU ST. JEAN WINERY

CHATEAU ST. JEAN WINERY
8555 Sonoma Hwy.
Kenwood, CA 95452
877-478-5326
chateaustjean.com

LOCATION: 8 miles east of Santa Rosa.

APPELLATION:
Sonoma Valley.

HOURS: 10 A.M.–5 P.M. daily, except major holidays.

TASTINGS: $15 in main Tasting Room; $20 for Saveur customized tasting; $25 in Reserve Tasting Room.

TOURS: Promenade Tour available, weather permitting. Visit chateaustjean.com for further information.

THE WINES: Cabernet Franc, Cabernet Sauvignon, Chardonnay, Fumé Blanc, Gewürztraminer, Malbec, Merlot, Pinot Blanc, Pinot Noir, Riesling, Syrah, Viognier.

SPECIALTIES: Cinq Cépages and vineyard-designated wines.

WINEMAKER:
Margo Van Staaveren.

ANNUAL PRODUCTION:
500,000 cases.

OF SPECIAL NOTE: Picnic tables in oak and redwood grove. Wine education classes. Store offering gourmet food and merchandise. Bocce ball court.

NEARBY ATTRACTION:
Sugarloaf Ridge State Park (hiking, camping, horseback riding).

With the dramatic profile of Sugarloaf Ridge as a backdrop, the exquisitely landscaped grounds at Chateau St. Jean Winery in Kenwood evoke the image of a grand country estate. The château itself dates to the 1920s, but it wasn't until 1973 that a family of Central Valley, California, growers of table grapes founded the winery. They named it after a favorite relative and, with tongue in cheek, placed a statue of "St. Jean" in the garden.

The winery building was constructed from the ground up to suit Chateau St. Jean's particular style of winemaking. The founders believed in the European practice of creating vineyard-designated wines, so they designed the winery to accommodate numerous lots of grapes, which could be kept separate throughout the winemaking process. Wines from each special vineyard are also bottled and marketed sepa- rately, with the vineyard name on the label. The winery makes a dozen vineyard-designated wines from the Sonoma Valley, Alexander Valley, Russian River Valley, and Carneros appella- tions. The winery also produces other premium varietals and one famously successful blend, the flagship Cinq Cépages Cabernet Sauvignon.

Chateau St. Jean became the first Sonoma winery to be awarded the prestigious Wine of the Year award from *Wine Spectator* magazine for its 1996 Cinq Cépages, a blend of the five traditional Bordeaux varietals, including Cabernet Sauvignon, Cabernet Franc, and Malbec. The winery received high acclaim again when it was given the #2 Wine of the Year award from *Wine Spectator* for its 1999 Cinq Cépages Cabernet Sauvignon. Winemaker Margo Van Staaveren has more than thirty years of vineyard and winemaking experience with Chateau St. Jean, and her knowledge of Sonoma further underscores her excellence in highlighting the best of each vineyard.

In the summer of 2000, Chateau St. Jean opened the doors to its new Visitor Center and Gardens. A formal Mediterranean-style garden contains roses, herbs, and citrus trees planted in oversized terra-cotta urns arranged to create a number of open-air "rooms." Visitors have always been welcome to relax on the winery's redwood-studded grounds, but now the setting is enhanced by the extensive garden plantings and a bocce ball court.

Beyond the Mediterranean garden is the tasting room with a custom-made tasting bar. Fashioned from mahogany with ebony accents, the thirty-five-foot-long bar is topped with sheet zinc. The elegant château houses the Reserve Tasting Room. Visitors who would like to learn more about Chateau St. Jean wines are encouraged to make a reservation for a more in-depth program.

DE LA MONTANYA WINERY & VINEYARDS

The road to De La Montanya Winery curves past the vineyards of Dry Creek Valley and under a rural bridge before arriving at the winery's understated entrance. The tranquil spot feels more like a hidden retreat than part of an active wine trail. Old barrels and farm equipment dotting informal flower beds and the barnlike winery enhance the farmyard flavor.

A simple door of knotty alder opens into the tasting room, a small space alive with country-kitchen friendliness. Faux antique hutches display bottled wine, and double doors with large glass panes offer a view into the attached winery. Tasters gather at the curved, Brazilian granite bar or head out to the patio, where seated tastings are poured on busy days. Zinfandel vines grow beside the patio, which has umbrella-shaded tables and a wood-fired pizza oven. Bordering the inti-mate space are beds of lavender, roses, and crape myrtle. A concrete path lined with tree roses and Zinfandel vines leads to a garden wonderland where visitors can relax. As inviting as a comfortable backyard, the lawn is set with redwood picnic tables. Nearby, a bocce ball court and a horseshoe pit are ready for play. Golden Delicious apple trees remaining from a 1950s-era orchard edge the grass. A new 2,000-square-foot barrel room nestled in the Felta Creek Vineyard features rustic redwood siding and a secluded patio decorated with inviting outdoor furniture. The winery hosts private afterhours tastings in the barrel room, with advance reservations.

Over the decades, Dry Creek Valley farmers have grown a variety of crops, from grapes in the late 1800s to walnuts, plums, apples, and, fueled by the 1970s wine boom, grapes again. Dennis De La Montanya decided to join their ranks in 1988, when a real estate appraisal he did alerted him to the value of wine grapes. Applying his experience in both banking and real estate, he started buying land with wine grapes in mind. He planted his first vineyard in 1994 and made his debut vintage, a Viognier, four years later.

De La Montanya farms 270 acres spanning six appellations and bottles eighteen different wines, some in lots as small as twenty-four cases. His popular Pin-Up series of red blends features labels bearing playfully provocative photographs of wine club members. Another series, the Finale, involves a partnership with a rock star. A descendant of French Huguenots who settled New Amsterdam in 1637, De La Montanya grew up on a cattle ranch in Marin County. He is a sixth-generation Californian who produces refined wines, while infusing a bit of the rambunctious West into his cheerful tasting room.

DE LA MONTANYA WINERY & VINEYARDS
999 Foreman Ln.
Healdsburg, CA 95448
707-433-3711
dennis@dlmwine.com
dlmwine.com

OWNERS: Dennis and Tina De La Montanya.

LOCATION: 3 miles southwest of Healdsburg.

APPELLATIONS: Sonoma Coast, Russian River Valley, Dry Creek Valley, Alexander Valley, Clear Lake, Kelseyville Bench.

HOURS: 11 A.M.–4:30 P.M. daily.

TASTINGS: $10 for 6–10 wines (applicable to purchase).

TOURS: By appointment.

THE WINES: Cabernet Sauvignon, Chardonnay, Gewürztraminer, Merlot, Petite Sirah, Pinot Noir, Sauvignon Blanc, Tempranillo, Viognier, Zinfandel.

SPECIALTIES: Vineyard-driven, small-lot wines, Bordeaux blends.

WINEMAKER: Tami Collins.

ANNUAL PRODUCTION: 5,000 cases.

OF SPECIAL NOTE: Wines are 90 percent estate grown and available only in tasting room. Large informal garden and picnic area with bocce ball and horseshoe pit. New barrel room available for private tastings paired with pizza prepared on-site.

NEARBY ATTRACTIONS: Russian River (swimming, canoeing, kayaking, rafting, fishing); Lake Sonoma (hiking, fishing, boating, camping, swimming).

DeLoach Vineyards

DeLoach Vineyards
1791 Olivet Rd.
Santa Rosa, CA 95401
707-755-3309
winestore@
deloachvineyards.com
deloachvineyards.com

Owner: Boisset Collection.

Location: Between River
Rd. and Guerneville Rd.

Appellation: Russian River
Valley.

Hours: 10 a.m.–5 p.m. daily.

Tastings: $15 for 5 wines.
Other tastings by appoint-
ment—$30 for 6 reserve
wines; $30 for Appellation
Tasting of 6 wines; $30 for
Royal Barrel Tasting; $30
for Wine and Cheese Pair-
ing; $35 for Les Libertine
Cellars Tasting; $40 for
Magic of Wine and Mustard;
$50 for Taste of Terroir;
$100 for M.F.S. Blending.

Tours: Daily at noon ($20,
includes tasting); self-
guided Theater of Nature
tour near vineyard (free).

The Wines: Chardonnay,
Pinot Noir, Pinot Noir Rosé,
Zinfandel.

Specialties: Vineyard-
designated Pinot Noirs,
Chardonnays, and
Zinfandels.

Winemaker: Brian Maloney.

Annual Production:
175,000 cases.

Of Special Note: Winery is
pet friendly. Picnic areas in
the terrace garden or in the
Estate Garden Grove. Picnic
baskets available for purchase by prior arrangement;
wood-fired pizza and wines
by the glass on summer
weekends. Cheese-and-wine
pairings daily by appointment. Vineyard-designated
and estate wines available
only in tasting room.

Nearby Attraction: Charles
M. Schulz Museum (exhib-
its on *Peanuts* creator and
other cartoonists).

As visitors step along a brick terrace leading to the DeLoach Vineyards tasting room, they pass a twenty-foot wooden sculpture of an ethereal woman reaching toward the sky and holding a child in the palm of a hand. The work, *Earth and Sky,* embodies DeLoach's dedication to biodynamic farming and environmental stewardship. The twenty-five-acre farm in the western Russian River Valley received organic certification in 2008 from the California Certi-fied Organic Farmers and biodynamic certification in 2009 from Demeter. Today the estate teems with life, in the vineyards and in a half-acre biodynamic garden where fragrant plants scent the air.

Although DeLoach is one of the region's oldest vine-yards, its sustainable prac-tices are relatively new. Cecil DeLoach planted Pinot Noir vines here in 1973 and helped establish the Russian River Valley AVA. In the early 2000s, Jean-Charles Boisset toured the area for the first time and instantly recognized the region's potential to create Pinot Noir wines to rival those from his native Burgundy. Boisset Family Estates purchased DeLoach Vineyards in 2003 and soon removed existing vineyards, replanted them with cover crops to revitalize the soil, and then planted new vines. In 2011 the winery released its first vintage made exclusively from estate grapes farmed with biodynamic techniques.

At DeLoach, guests can choose from among an impressive array of tastings, themed activi-ties, and tours in various venues. They may taste limited-release, vineyard-designated wines at the composite-stone bar in the tasting salon, at picnic tables on the terrace, or in Les Libertine Cellars, decorated in the style of the seventeenth- and eighteenth-century French royal court. Within the ultra-chic tasting hall of sister winery JCB, visitors sample Jean-Charles Boisset's elegant, limited-production wines from Burgundy and California. Held in a private guest house, Taste of Terroir is a rare opportunity to compare Boisset Collection wines from France with their California counter-parts. DeLoach partners with famed French mustard producer Fallot to offer a garden tour followed by mustard making and wine tasting, paired with mustard-inspired foods. Yet another option is a blending seminar in which participants wear French winemaker berets and aprons and craft a bottle of Pinot Noir to take home.

On tours of the vineyards and biodynamic garden, visitors explore exhibits that illustrate and explain DeLoach's organic and biodynamic farming philosophy. They are welcome to picnic at shaded tables in the lush backyard grove. Goats, chickens, and other farm animals in the adjacent yard fill the air with musical chatter—all part of DeLoach's vibrant biodynamic ecosystem.

DUTCHER CROSSING WINERY

Dutcher Crossing Winery exemplifies the low-key ambience of Dry Creek Valley, an appellation sixteen miles long and at most two miles across that has been home to generations of grape growers and winemakers. Sited at a scenic junction of two creeks — Dry Creek and Dutcher Creek — the small winery has a quaint charm, and its architecture evokes the look of the farming community that first flourished here in the early 1900s. A wide breezeway between the tasting room and the winemaking building offers panoramic views of the valley's hillside beauty.

Purchased by Debra Mathy in 2007, Dutcher Crossing produces small-lot, vineyard-designated wines crafted by winemaker Kerry Damskey. In addition to the signature Cabernet Sauvignon–Syrah blend, he makes several Dry Creek Valley Zinfandels, select Chardonnays from the Alexander Valley, and Pinot Noir sourced from the Russian River Valley. Over his thirty years as a winemaker, Damskey has become a leading proponent of blending; his Cabernet Sauvignon–Syrah is the first wine of its kind in Dry Creek Valley.

Proprietor Mathy expressed her adventuresome side by planting an estate vineyard block in the Châteauneuf-du-Pape style: a selection of Rhône varieties such as Grenache, Syrah, Mourvèdre, Cinsault, and Counoise. Guests can sip their selections while overlooking this planting from the trellised picnic area, set amid colorful gardens. Views of the valley landscape are also visible through the tall windows in the spacious tasting room, where highlights include a vaulted beam ceiling, a polished limestone tasting bar, and wide hickory plank floors. At one end of the rectangular room, a cozy conversation area with comfortable seating faces a fireplace made from locally quarried stone and topped with a mantel fashioned from distressed railroad ties. A vintage bicycle, the icon chosen to grace the redesigned Dutcher Crossing wine label, is also on display. It is a replica of the 1892 Rudge crafted in the classic Penny Farthing style so that the front wheel is larger than the back.

Debra Mathy considers the bicycle a symbol of the timeless qualities of an artisan approach to life as well as to winemaking. As the last Christmas present she received from her late father, it also represents her journey to find Dutcher Crossing Winery. Mathy, an avid cyclist and lover of bicycles since childhood, spent ten years traveling with her father to discover the winery of their dreams. She can almost always be found during the day greeting visitors, with her golden lab, Dutchess, at her side. Their friendliness and enthusiasm reflect the culture and spirit of Dutcher Crossing.

DUTCHER CROSSING WINERY
8533 Dry Creek Rd.
Geyserville, CA 95441
707-431-2700
866-431-2711
info@dutchercrossing
winery.com
dutchercrossingwinery
.com

OWNER: Debra Mathy.

LOCATION: 8.5 miles west of Dry Creek Valley exit off U.S. 101 via Dry Creek Rd.

APPELLATION: Dry Creek Valley.

HOURS: 11 A.M.–5 P.M. daily.

TASTINGS: $5 for 4-wine flight; $10 for reserve wine flight.

TOURS: ATV vineyard tours by appointment.

THE WINES: Cabernet Sauvignon, Chardonnay, Merlot, Petite Sirah, Port, Sauvignon Blanc, Syrah, Zinfandel.

SPECIALTY: Zinfandel.

WINEMAKER: Kerry Damskey.

ANNUAL PRODUCTION: 9,000 cases.

OF SPECIAL NOTE: Picnic tables (reservations for parties of six or more) and *pétanque* court. Select wines sold only at tasting room.

NEARBY ATTRACTION: Lake Sonoma (swimming, fishing, boating, hiking, camping).

FRANCIS FORD COPPOLA WINERY

**FRANCIS FORD COPPOLA
WINERY**
300 Via Archimedes
Geyserville, CA 95441
707-857-1471
guestservices@
francisfordcoppolawinery
.com
francisfordcoppolawinery
.com

OWNER: Francis Ford
Coppola.

LOCATION: 6 miles northwest
of downtown Healdsburg.

APPELLATIONS: Alexander
Valley, Dry Creek Valley,
Sonoma Coast, Sonoma
Valley, Russian River Valley.

HOURS: 11 A.M.–6 P.M. daily.

TASTINGS: $10; $20 for 4
Sonoma County wines.
By appointment: $20 for
Bottling Ballet Mechanique
(held in bottling facility);
$60 for Wine, Whim & Song
(tasting accompanied by
music); $75 for Tasting in
the Dark (blind tasting).

TOURS: None.

THE WINES: Cabernet Sau-
vignon, Chardonnay, Late
Harvest Semillon, Malbec,
Merlot, Moscato, Petite
Sirah, Pinot Grigio, Pinot
Noir, Riesling, Rosé, Sauvi-
gnon Blanc, Shiraz, Syrah,
Viognier, Zinfandel.

SPECIALTY: Archimedes
(Bordeaux-style blend).

WINEMAKER: Corey Beck.

ANNUAL PRODUCTION:
Unavailable.

OF SPECIAL NOTE: Winery
is family friendly. Two restaurants: poolside café and
Rustic, open daily for lunch
and dinner. Movie gallery,
extensive retail shop, swimming pool, performance
pavilion, bocce courts.
Annual events include an
Easter Egg Hunt and Hal-
loween Carnival.

In his youth, film director Francis Ford Coppola visited Tivoli Gardens amusement park in Copenhagen—a wonderland with theater pavilions, rides, cafés, and lush gardens for everyone to enjoy. When he and his family purchased the historic Château Souverain property in Sonoma County just north of the town of Healdsburg in 2006, he decided to create a similar wonderland at his new estate. Coppola worked with Academy Award–winning production designer Dean Tavoularis on the property design, drawing much inspiration from Tivoli Gardens. They planned a destination winery for the whole family, where adults could taste wine and people of all ages could enjoy food, music, dancing, games, swimming, and performances.

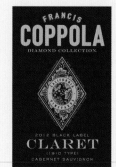

In 2010 Coppola unveiled the completely refurbished and expanded Francis Ford Coppola Winery estate. The sprawling com-plex includes two tasting rooms, two restaurants, a performing arts pavilion, two swimming pools connected by a swim-through water bridge, a sunbathing ter-race, twenty-eight European-style cabana changing rooms, a teepee holding a lending library of chil-dren's books, and a landscaped park area with lawns, game tables, and four regulation-sized bocce courts. Displays of authentic mem-orabilia from Coppola's films appear in a dedicated gallery and throughout the property.

Coppola also revitalized and expanded the winemaking facilities, bottling line, and vineyards, working alongside director of winemaking and general manager Corey Beck, a Calistoga native with more than twenty years' experience in the wine industry. The winery's portfolio now features nearly a dozen distinct brands; the top tier includes Francis Coppola Reserve, Director's Cut, and Director's, showcasing Sonoma County appellations and vineyards. Archimedes, the flagship wine, is a highly complex blend of the best barrels within each lot of Cabernet Sauvignon and Cabernet Franc, from the estate and other vineyards in the Alexander Valley and Knights Valley AVAs. It pays homage to Francis Ford Coppola's Uncle Archimedes, named for the Greek mathematician.

Visitors can taste Archimedes and other wines inside the two-story hospitality center. Special focus flights include a tasting where blindfolded guests sample wines in a dark, private room; a wine tasting to the accompaniment of different music selections; and a seasonal children's smoothie tasting. On Tuesday *a tavola* nights, the restaurant servers dress in vintage Italian costumes and portray a traditional Italian family—all part of Coppola's vision of creating a fun, festive destination for all ages.

GARY FARRELL VINEYARDS AND WINERY

Meandering Westside Road traces the course of the Russian River through aromatic redwood groves and past some of the region's oldest and most prestigious vineyards. The northern end of Westside, closer to Healdsburg, is lined with wineries, but down near Wohler Road, on the outskirts of leafy Forestville, most structures are likely to be residences. There is little to prepare travelers for the dramatic entrance to Gary Farrell Winery, where a sharp turn leads up a steep driveway that climbs past native live oaks and an impressive stand of towering redwoods.

Winery founder Gary Farrell opened his eponymous facility in 2000, high on a ridge overlooking a bewitching slice of the Russian River appellation, famed for outstanding Pinot Noir and Chardonnay. Farrell made his first vintage in 1982, producing fifty cases of Pinot Noir from the nearby Rochioli and Allen vineyards, two highly regarded estates. He was among the first to recognize the world-class potential of Russian River Valley fruit. In the early 1980s, most area grapes disappeared into nameless blends, but when Farrell, along with such local pioneers as Davis Bynum, Joe Rochioli, and Tom Dehlinger, started making stellar wine, they ignited the region's fame. Farrell forged lasting relationships with like-minded visionaries. As a result, thirty years on, the winery has access to fruit from some of the region's most coveted vineyards, including Rochioli, Bacigalupi, and Ritchie.

Located well off the beaten path, the winery sits at an elevation of four hundred feet, but the steep slopes create the illusion of a much higher vantage point. Visitors enter the winery beneath a sculptural redwood arbor, and about two steps inside the tasting room, they are likely to simply stop and gape at the sweeping vista of madrones, valley oaks, and redwoods visible through wall-to-wall picture windows behind the tasting bar. The ambience is woodsy yet refined, with little to distract from experiencing the wines, which are small-production, single-vineyard Pinot Noir and Chardonnay that epitomize the best of the Russian River Valley appellation.

Tastings range from a casual sampling at the bar to a hosted, seated experience that often includes one or two library pours. All take place in view of the redwoods that define this part of the world, where ribbons of fog can often be seen drifting through the forested valley below. Here, close to the wines' source, visitors are imbued with a visceral memory of how the Russian River Valley influences the wine in the glass.

GARY FARRELL VINEYARDS AND WINERY
10701 Westside Rd.
Healdsburg, CA 95448
707-473-2909
concierge@
garyfarrellwinery.com
garyfarrellwinery.com

FOUNDER: Gary Farrell.

LOCATION: 12 miles southwest of downtown Healdsburg, near Wohler Bridge.

APPELLATION: Russian River Valley.

HOURS: 10:30 A.M.–4:30 P.M. daily.

TASTINGS: $15–$35. Reservations recommended (required for groups of 7 or more).

TOURS: By appointment.

THE WINES: Chardonnay, Pinot Noir, Sauvignon Blanc, Zinfandel.

SPECIALTIES: Vineyard-designated Chardonnay and Pinot Noir.

WINEMAKER: Theresa Heredia.

ANNUAL PRODUCTION: 25,000 cases.

OF SPECIAL NOTE: Terrace Tasting offers sweeping views of Russian River Valley. Original art by local artists for purchase. Limited-production wines available only from winery.

NEARBY ATTRACTIONS: Russian River (rafting, fishing, swimming, canoeing, kayaking); Armstrong Redwoods State Natural Reserve (hiking, horseback riding).

GLORIA FERRER CAVES & VINEYARDS

**GLORIA FERRER
CAVES & VINEYARDS**
23555 Hwy. 121
Sonoma, CA 95476
707-933-1917
info@gloriaferrer.com
gloriaferrer.com

OWNERS: Ferrer family.

LOCATION: 4 miles south of the town of Sonoma.

APPELLATION: Los Carneros.

HOURS: 10 A.M.–5 P.M. daily.

TASTINGS: $6–$16 per glass of sparkling wine; $7–$13 for estate varietal wine; $18–$33 for flights.

TOURS: Public tours available three times a day. Private tours by appointment.

THE WINES: Blanc de Noirs, Sonoma Brut, Va de Vi sparkling wines; Carneros Pinot Noir, Chardonnay, Merlot.

SPECIALTIES: Carneros Cuvée, Extra Brut, Brut Rosé, Anniversary Cuvée, Blanc de Blancs, Royal Cuvée sparkling wines; José S. Ferrer and WillMar Pinot Noirs.

WINEMAKERS: Bob Iantosca and Steven Urberg.

ANNUAL PRODUCTION: 120,000 cases.

OF SPECIAL NOTE: Tours include cave views. Winery produces several small-lot Pinot Noirs.

NEARBY ATTRACTIONS: Mission San Francisco Solano, Lachryma Montis (Mariano Vallejo's estate), and other historic buildings in downtown Sonoma; Sonoma Raceway (NASCAR and other events); biplane flights; Cornerstone Sonoma (garden installations and tours).

The Carneros appellation, with its continual winds and cool marine air, is known far and wide as an ideal climate for growing Pinot Noir and Chardonnay grapes. The word spread all the way to Spain, where the Ferrer family had been making sparkling wine for more than a century. The Ferrers are the world's largest producer of sparkling wine.

Members of the family had been looking for vineyard land in the United States off and on for fifty years when José and Gloria Ferrer visited the southern part of the Sonoma Valley. The climate reminded them of their Catalan home in Spain, and in 1982 they acquired a forty-acre pasture and then, four years later, another two hundred acres nearby. They started planting vineyards with

traditional sparkling wine grapes. The winery now cultivates nearly four hundred acres in Carneros and, in addition to sparkling wines, produces estate varietals, including Pinot Noir, Merlot, and Chardonnay. Gloria Ferrer wines have a history of critical success. Within a year of its 1986 debut, the winery won seven gold medals, marking the beginning of many accolades to come. Since the winery opened, the wines have received more than 700 gold medals.

The winery that José Ferrer built was the first sparkling wine house in Carneros. Named for his wife, it was inspired by the Ferrer family's eleventh-century farmhouse in Sant Sadurni d'Anoia, Spain, complete with red tile roofs and expansive views. Complementing the exterior, the many windows allow guests to view the winery's Carneros vineyards from every angle. The ties to Spain continue in the market area, which offers a selection of Spanish meats, cheeses, and spiced almonds to pair with the sparkling wine, as well as cookbooks and the necessary ingredients for preparing tapas and paella at home. Various chocolates are filled with Gloria Ferrer sparkling and varietal wines.

Visitors are welcome to enjoy Gloria Ferrer wines, both sparkling and estate varietals, in the spacious tasting room or outside on the Vista Terrace. There they are treated to a breathtaking view of Carneros and the upper reaches of San Pablo Bay. On a clear day, they can see all the way to the peak of 3,848-foot Mount Diablo in the East Bay. Sparkling wines and barrels of estate varietals are aged in the caves tunneled into the hillside behind the visitor center.

Tours of the winery include a visit to these aromatic dark recesses, where guides explain the traditional *méthode champenoise* process of creating sparkling wine, during which the wine undergoes its secondary fermentation in the bottle—the one that forms the characteristic bubbles.

HARTFORD FAMILY WINERY

Toyon, oak, and coast redwood fringe the sinuous country road that leads to the home of Hartford Family Winery. At the driveway, a one-lane bridge crosses Green Valley Creek into a forest clearing where the château-style winery offers a peaceful retreat. Sycamores shade the stately complex, and a fountain bubbles opposite the double doors of the tasting room. Furnished with European antiques, the spacious foyer opens into a space with crisp white cabinetry and a French limestone floor.

Renowned for crafting single-vineyard Chardonnay, Pinot Noir, and old-vine Zinfandel, the winery was founded in 1993 by Don and Jennifer Hartford. Don, whose family farmed strawberries in western Massachusetts, had recently concluded a success-ful law practice in Northern California and was drawn to the viticulture of Russian River Valley. With help from Jennifer's father, Jess Jackson, cofounder of Kendall-Jackson Wine Estates, the couple pur-chased the winery property about a dozen miles northwest of Santa Rosa.

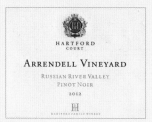

Of the winery's thirteen Pinot Noir offerings, eleven are strikingly diverse single-vineyard bottlings made from 95 percent estate fruit. The estate vineyards thrive in five appellations: Los Carneros, Anderson Valley, Sonoma Coast, Russian River Valley, and Green Valley. All are cool-climate sites that yield small crops of often late-ripening grapes treasured for their flawless varietal flavors. The blended Land's Edge Pinot Noir is sourced from estate vineyards located in Annapolis, on the Sonoma coast, some thirty miles north of the tasting room. For Chardonnay, the winery turns to the Sonoma Coast and Russian River Valley appellations. About 90 percent of the fruit is harvested from estate vineyards, including Fog Dance Vineyard, in the Green Valley AVA, and Seascape Vineyard, a six-acre ridgetop site facing Bodega Bay. The Hartfords craft five single-vineyard and one blended Zinfandel, all from dry-farmed Russian River Valley vines boasting an average age of a hundred-plus years. The grapes from these august vines exhibit rich berry and spice components borne of both the vines' great age and the region's relatively chilly, protracted growing season.

The single-vineyard wines are made in limited lots, some as small as a hundred cases. During harvest, all the fruit is handpicked and then sorted by hand to remove everything but the best berries. Using only French oak barrels, the winemaker selects from nineteen different cooperages, matching barrels to each lot of wine to elevate the expression of both vineyard site and varietal characteristics.

HARTFORD FAMILY WINERY
8075 Martinelli Rd.
Forestville, CA 95436
707-887-8030
800-588-0234, ext. 1
info@hartfordwines.com
hartfordwines.com

OWNERS: Don and Jennifer Hartford.

LOCATION: 2 miles northwest of Forestville.

APPELLATION: Russian River Valley.

HOURS: 10 A.M.–4:30 P.M. daily.

TASTINGS: $15 for 6 wines; $40 for Seated Private Library Tasting of 6 wines; $35–$40 for boxed lunch and signature flight. Reservations required.

TOURS: None.

THE WINES: Chardonnay, Pinot Noir, Zinfandel.

SPECIALTIES: Single-vineyard Chardonnay, Pinot Noir, and old-vine Zinfandel.

WINEMAKER: Jeff Stewart.

ANNUAL PRODUCTION: 12,000–15,000 cases.

OF SPECIAL NOTE: Shaded picnic area with tables. Zinfandel Port and most single-vineyard wines available only in tasting room. Second tasting room located at 331 Healdsburg Ave., Healdsburg, open 10 A.M.–5:30 P.M. daily.

NEARBY ATTRACTIONS: Russian River (rafting, fishing, swimming, canoeing, kayaking); Armstrong Redwoods State Reserve (hiking, horseback riding); Laguna de Santa Rosa (freshwater wetlands with wildlife viewing).

J VINEYARDS & WINERY

J VINEYARDS & WINERY
11447 Old Redwood Hwy.
Healdsburg, CA 95448
888-594-6326
info@jwine.com
jwine.com

OWNER: Judy Jordan.

LOCATION: 3 miles south of
Healdsburg Plaza.

APPELLATION: Russian River
Valley.

HOURS: 11 A.M.–5 P.M. daily.

TASTINGS: $20 for 5 wines;
$30 for 5 still or sparkling
wines in the Legacy Reserve
Lounge (reservations sug-
gested); $45 for 4 wines
served on the terrace
seasonally; $75 for 6 wines
paired with five-course
meal in the Bubble Room
(reservations suggested).

TOURS: 11:30 A.M. and
2:30 P.M. daily ($30).

THE WINES: Chardonnay,
Pinot Gris, Pinot Meunier,
Pinot Noir, Pinotage,
sparkling wine, Vin Gris,
Viognier.

SPECIALTIES: *Méthode
champenoise* sparkling wine,
Pinot Gris, single-vineyard
Pinot Noir.

WINEMAKER:
Melissa Stackhouse.

ANNUAL PRODUCTION:
100,000 cases.

OF SPECIAL NOTE: Gift
shop with jams, olive oils,
candles, jewelry, wine-
glasses, Champagne flutes,
and other wine-related
items. Pink Party for release
of Brut Rosé sparkling wine
(August). Most wines made
from estate-grown grapes.
Single-vineyard Pinot
Noirs, estate Pinot Gris, and
small-production sparkling
wines available only at tasting room.

NEARBY ATTRACTIONS:
Riverfront Regional Park;
Healdsburg Museum and
Historical Society.

Just before the first fork in the dusty former main highway that slices south from central Healdsburg, a large sign bearing a calligraphic yellow "J" marks the location of J Vineyards & Winery. Simple yet sophisticated, with a faintly frothy plume, the letter, owner Judy Jordan's first and last initial, hints at the poise and pluck that underlie this Russian River Valley pioneer's winemaking endeavors, and her hospitality as well.

In the mid-1980s when Europe's Champagne houses were staking their California claims, Judy Jordan, the daughter of the founders of Jordan Vineyard & Winery, opened a small operation focusing on sparkling wines made from Russian River Valley Chardonnay and Pinot Noir. With her J Vintage Brut, Jordan established her winery's reputation and within a decade had purchased from Sonoma the flagship prop- erty J still occupies.

RUSSIAN RIVER VALLEY
PINOT NOIR

J VINEYARDS
ESTATE GROWN

Even before this acquisi- tion, Jordan had begun buck- ing another tradition—that sparkling winemakers can't also triumph in the market for still wines—branching out into Pinot Noir, Pinot Gris, and Chardonnay. Jordan holds a degree in earth sciences and geology, training that served her well as she sought out the best vineyards, soils, and microclimates to nurture Pinot Noir. The scientist in the vintner may have inspired experiments, both successful, with the varietals Pinot Meunier and Pinotage, the latter a South African hybrid of Pinot Noir and Cinsault so rare in California that J's 2.8 acres of vines represent more than a quarter of the state's plantings.

Jordan's forays into sparkling and still wines can be explored on an engaging sip-while-you-see tour that takes in two vineyards, the crush pad, and the aging cellar before a stop in the casual-chic Legacy Reserve Lounge. The room's floor-to-ceiling windows provide views of the production area below, where, especially on weekdays, bottling and other activities often take place. Well-versed pourers recount a briefer version of the J story in the Signature Bar tasting area, whose focal point is a massive stained-steel installation by Napa-based artist Gordon Huether. Fiber-optic filaments set behind the piece's glass elements create a twinkling effect that mimics sparkling-wine bubbles.

At this winery with a setting for sipping for nearly all moods, tastings also take place in the Legacy Reserve Lounge and on a sunny terrace edged by a stream. The pièce de résistance, though, is the fetchingly contemporary Bubble Room, where composed dishes prepared on-site by executive chef Erik Johnson, formerly of Healdsburg's Dry Creek Kitchen restaurant, are paired with J wines. J was among the first wineries to introduce gourmet food-and-wine pairings, and its rendition remains among Northern California's best.

JORDAN VINEYARD & WINERY

A sense of change amid permanence prevails at Jordan Vineyard & Winery, where the son of its founders has honored their legacy by adding new luster to this Alexander Valley icon. John Jordan was still a boy when his parents, Tom and Sally Jordan, established a reputation for meticulous winemaking. From the start, the couple took the high road, hiring André Tchelistcheff, Napa Valley's most esteemed winemaker in the 1970s, as their consulting enologist. To design their château and winery, they brought in the San Francisco architectural firm of Backen, Arrigoni & Ross, whose later projects included filmmaker George Lucas's Skywalker Ranch.

With its classic carmine doors and shutters, the château serves as a visual metaphor for the Jordan winemaking phi- losophy, which in the French tradition emphasizes balance, elegance, and food affinity. It is by design that Jordan Cabernet Sauvignons and Chardonnays grace the wine lists of many top restaurants. As was the case when the château was com- pleted in 1976, the wines are still crafted by Rob Davis, the Jordans' original winemaker, but numerous initiatives under- taken by John Jordan since he took the winery's helm in 2005 have reenergized both the winemaking and the hospitality. A rigorous soil-mapping study led to more row-specific and even vine-specific farming practices, and solar power, composting, and other sustainable practices were introduced.

Visitors to Jordan can learn about its wines and history at tastings and on tours. Depending on the chosen tour, guests visit a wood-paneled private library and its cleverly hidden adjoining room, taste current and library wines as well as extra-virgin olive oil made from estate-grown olives, and sample small bites created by longtime executive chef Todd Knoll. The Winery Tour visits part of the château and passes by massive, highly sculptural oak tanks.

On the splurge-worthy Estate Tour and Tasting, participants sample fine pastries and briefly visit the winery before a Mercedes coach whisks them to an organic garden on the nearly 1,200-acre estate to view and taste the impressive produce. A lakeside oak grove is the setting for Chardonnays and light morsels, and a hilltop vista point provides an appropriately dramatic venue for tasting a current and a library Cabernet Sauvignon, matched with cheeses and a small meat or vegetarian dish. John Jordan himself often joins the three-hour excursion at the vista point, further enhancing the impression that one has been welcomed onto an exclusive country estate.

JORDAN VINEYARD & WINERY
1474 Alexander Valley Rd.
Healdsburg, CA 95448
707-431-5250
800-654-1213
info@jordanwinery.com
jordanwinery.com

OWNER: John Jordan.

LOCATION: About 4 miles northeast of Healdsburg.

APPELLATION: Alexander Valley.

HOURS: 8 A.M.–4 P.M. Monday–Friday; 9 A.M.– 3:30 P.M. Saturday; 9 A.M.–3:30 P.M. Sunday mid-April–mid-November.

TASTINGS: $30 for Library Tasting of 3 wines, by appointment.

TOURS: Winery Tour and Library Tasting ($40) daily year-round. Estate Tour and Tasting ($120) Thursday–Monday mid-April–mid-November. Both by appointment.

THE WINES: Cabernet Sauvignon, Chardonnay.

SPECIALTIES: Alexander Valley Cabernet Sauvignon, Russian River Chardonnay.

WINEMAKER: Rob Davis.

ANNUAL PRODUCTION: 100,000 cases.

OF SPECIAL NOTE: Extensive landscaped grounds and gardens, including Tuscan olive trees. Jordan estate extra-virgin olive oil sold at winery. Same winemaker since 1976. Library and large-format wines available only at winery.

NEARBY ATTRACTIONS: Lake Sonoma (boating, camping, fishing, hiking, swimming); Jimtown Store (country market, homemade foods).

Keller Estate

Keller Estate
5875 Lakeville Hwy.
Petaluma, CA 94954
707-765-2117
kellerestate.com

Owners: Keller family.

Location: 7 miles southeast of downtown Petaluma.

Appellation: Sonoma Coast.

Hours: 11 A.M.–4 P.M. Friday–Sunday for walk-ins; Monday–Thursday by appointment (same-day appointments available).

Tastings: Sit-down tastings; $20 for 5 wines.

Tours: Estate tour and tasting in reserve room ($60), 11:30 A.M. and 2 P.M., Friday and Saturday, by appointment.

The Wines: Chardonnay, Pinot Gris, Pinot Noir, Rotie (Rhône blend).

Specialties: Single-vineyard Chardonnay and Pinot Noir.

Winemaker: Alex Holman.

Annual Production: 5,000 cases.

Of Special Note: All wines and olive oil are estate grown. Wine pairings with cheese and charcuterie available. Vintage car from owner's collection on display. Winery is pet friendly.

Nearby Attractions: Shollenberger Park (hiking, bird-watching); San Pablo Bay National Wildlife Refuge (hiking, fishing, interpretive program); Sonoma Raceway (NASCAR and other events).

White rail fences frame the road to Keller Estate, an architectural gem set among the windswept pastures and wetlands bordering the Petaluma River. The 650-acre property rests in the Petaluma Gap, an up-and-coming part of the Sonoma Coast appellation, where breezes off San Pablo Bay can whip through at fifty miles per hour. The region receives ample sunshine, however, which prompted Deborah and Arturo Keller to plant thirteen acres of Chardonnay in 1989.

By 2000 the Kellers, with help from Arturo's daughter, Ana, had begun transforming the appellation's southernmost winery into a superior wine estate. They expanded their thirteen-acre vineyard to ninety acres of Chardonnay

and Pinot Noir, as well as some Syrah, Viognier, and Pinot Gris. As director of the winery, Ana ensured a diversity of fruit for the all-estate-grown wine by planting vineyard blocks throughout the property. The land around the blocks retains its open-range look, save for 2,000 olive trees planted for making olive oil.

Built in 2003, the winery is an arresting low-profile structure of straight lines and gentle curves. It was designed by the late Ricardo Legoretta, an acclaimed Mexican architect famed for his playful use of light, color, and geometric forms. Covering the exterior are quarried stones—some bearing fossils and even tombstone engravings—salvaged from a Chinese village in advance of flooding for the Three Gorges Dam. From the flat roof rise a cylinder and a volcano-like cone that funnel sunshine into the cellar. Inside, these skylights glow like giant yellow polka dots, as decorative as they are functional.

Originally from Mexico, Arturo Keller is an automotive manufacturer and avid collector of vintage automobiles. Antique cars drew him to the Petaluma area, where he found a hub of fellow aficionados.

The atmosphere at Keller is relaxed and engaging as tasters admire southerly views of the Petaluma Gap and 2,571-foot Mount Tamalpais in Marin County. San Francisco lies at the horizon, about thirty-five miles away. Once part of the ancient seabed of San Pablo Bay, the region's diverse soils lend a unified thread of lively minerality to the wines. Seated tastings are poured on a broad patio with teak furniture grouped under wisteria-laden arbors. The tasting room is a Spanish Colonial blend of warm-hued wood and local stone. Doors at the back open into a four-hundred-foot-long, cement-walled cave holding more than two hundred oak barrels. Cellar workers have painted bands of crimson stain on the barrels reserved for red wine, lending ribbons of jewel tones to the shadowy cave.

LAMBERT BRIDGE WINERY

Surrounded by the lush vineyards and rolling hills of the Dry Creek Valley, Lambert Bridge Winery offers a setting for all seasons. In spring, the hillside is yellow with daffodils. By summer, the decades-old wisteria vines clinging to the porch and roof render a profusion of aromatic lavender blossoms. From then until late fall, the weather is perfect for picnicking in the Mediterranean-style gardens. And as winter's wet chill descends, a roaring blaze in a huge granite hearth fills the high-ceilinged tasting room with welcoming warmth.

The site once belonged to the C. L. Lambert Ranch, a large parcel that included farmland as well as a school, a store, and a trestle bridge across Dry Creek. The Lambert Bridge, dating to 1920, is now the only single-lane public bridge in the valley. When Lambert Bridge Winery opened in 1975, it was only the second winery to be built in Dry Creek Valley since Prohibition. Today Bordeaux varietals and blends take center stage in the winery's portfolio. The winemaking team is headed by veteran winemaker and Sonoma County native Jennifer Higgins, whose twenty-plus years of experience include stints at William Hill Winery in Napa and Alexander Valley's Lancaster Estate.

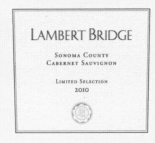

LAMBERT BRIDGE

SONOMA COUNTY
CABERNET SAUVIGNON

LIMITED SELECTION
2010

Starting with the harvest of 2005, Lambert Bridge began using an elaborate new collection of technologically advanced equipment that allows the sorting and selection of wine grapes down to the individual berries. Only completely mature, perfectly formed grapes are hand-selected for the wines. The process is so time-intensive that few wineries use it, but Lambert Bridge finds that the improvement in quality more than justifies the extra effort. About 60 percent of the grapes come from four estate vineyards in Sonoma County, and include the Winery Ranch and Meyers vineyards that surround the Lambert Bridge Winery tasting room. Other estate vineyards are the seven-acre Gilfillan Vineyard at 1,100 feet in elevation in the Moon Mountain District and the thirty-acre Chambers Vineyard east of the Russian River. The remaining fruit is sourced from local growers who farm to the Lambert Bridge winemaking team's stringent specifications.

The tasting room features a redwood bar fronted in hand-hammered copper. It is a close match to the twelve-foot-long reserve tasting bar in the adjacent barrel room. Here soaring redwood ceilings and glowing candlelight establish a fitting ambience for a private sampling of limited-production wines paired with locally sourced artisanal foods. Visitors can also enjoy picnicking with wine and food at teak tables on a sloping lawn, surrounded by ancient redwoods, lavish garden, and sweeping views of the Dry Creek Valley.

LAMBERT BRIDGE WINERY
4085 W. Dry Creek Rd.
Healdsburg, CA 95448
707-431-9600
wines@lambertbridge.com
lambertbridge.com

OWNER: Patti Chambers.

LOCATION: About 6.5 miles northwest of Healdsburg via Dry Creek Rd.

APPELLATION: Dry Creek Valley.

HOURS: 10:30 A.M.–4:30 P.M. daily.

TASTINGS: $15 for 5 wines; $25 for 5 reserve wines; $45 for 5 wines paired with food.

TOURS: Seasonal harvest tours.

THE WINES: Cabernet Franc, Cabernet Sauvignon, Chardonnay, Malbec, Merlot, Petit Verdot, Petite Sirah, Sauvignon Blanc, Viognier, Zinfandel.

SPECIALTIES: Limited Selection Cabernet, Crane Creek Cuvée (Merlot, Cabernet Sauvignon).

WINEMAKER: Jennifer Higgins.

ANNUAL PRODUCTION: 8,000 cases.

OF SPECIAL NOTE: Picnic tables and gardens. Local cheeses and artisanal charcuterie available on-site. Food-and-wine pairings Friday–Sunday by appointment. Annual events include Passport to Dry Creek Valley (April). Bottle limits on Crane Creek Cuvée.

NEARBY ATTRACTION: Lake Sonoma (boating, hiking, camping).

LEDSON WINERY & VINEYARDS

LEDSON WINERY & VINEYARDS
7335 Hwy. 12
Kenwood, CA 95409
707-537-3810
ledson.com

OWNER:
Steve Noble Ledson.

LOCATION: About 2 miles northwest of the town of Kenwood.

APPELLATIONS: Napa Valley, Sonoma Valley, Mendocino.

HOURS: 10 A.M.–5 P.M. daily.

TASTINGS: $15, $20, and $25; $50 for private wine and cheese tasting.

TOURS: By appointment.

THE WINES: Barbera, Cabernet Franc, Cabernet Sauvignon, Carignane, Chardonnay, Malbec, Petit Verdot, Petite Syrah, Pinot Noir, Sangiovese, Sauvignon Blanc, Syrah, Zinfandel.

SPECIALTIES: Limited-production classic and unusual varietals.

WINEMAKER:
Steve Noble Ledson.

ANNUAL PRODUCTION:
Fewer than 25,000 cases.

OF SPECIAL NOTE: Ledson Hotel and Centre du Vin, hotel and restaurant, located on Sonoma Plaza. Wines available only at winery, online, and to guests of the hotel and restaurant.

NEARBY ATTRACTIONS:
Hood Mountain Regional Park (hiking, biking); Sugarloaf Ridge State Park (hiking).

A distinctive blend of winemaking artistry, family passion, and unparalleled hospitality, Ledson Winery & Vineyards pays homage to the Ledson family's 150-year history of grape growing and winemaking. Owner/winemaker Steve Ledson—who can often be found pouring wines and greeting visitors at the winery—puts a premium on crafting both world-class wines and a world-class visitor experience. Ledson personally trains each wine presenter to ensure that guests enjoy an engaging and informative tasting tailored to their individual preferences.

The stunning French Normandy–inspired Ledson estate—known worldwide as "the castle"—features a number of small, intimate tasting bars and private salons where guests can sample Ledson's limited-production vineyard-designated and appellation-specific wines, learn about the family's sustainable grape-growing and winemaking practices, and soak up local history and lore from the friendly and knowledgeable staff. Tasters can choose from a menu of sampling options or make arrangements for a private winemaker tasting for groups as small as two and up to ten, paired with artisan cheese and charcuterie.

The family's history of farming in the area dates back to the 1860s. Steve Ledson's great-great-grandfather on his father's side was an early pioneer in Sonoma County winemaking, and both sets of grandparents had worked adjoining Sonoma Valley ranches. The family had grown grapes for years, so Steve, the fifth generation to farm in the area, jumped at the chance to buy the twenty-one-acre property. When the Ledson family started construction in 1992, they thought the property would be ideal for their residence. They planted Merlot vineyards, and given the quality of the grape harvests, Steve Ledson decided to turn the architectural showpiece into a winery and tasting room. In 1997 he released his first wine: the 1994 Estate Merlot. The winery opened five years later.

In addition to exploring an array of wine-tasting options, visitors can browse the beautifully appointed estate and grounds; shop for luxury wine accessories, apparel, and home goods at the extensive gift boutique; and savor locally grown and produced epicurean delights at the Gourmet Marketplace and Deli. Whether picking up a taste of Sonoma to bring home or putting together the perfect lunch to complement their Ledson wine, guests can choose from a tempting selection of gourmet meats, artisan cheeses, fresh-baked breads, made-to-order sandwiches, salads, and desserts. They can then enjoy lunch outdoors in the hundred-year-old oak grove overlooking the estate vineyards and water fountains, or indoors in the intimate parlor with its elegant Italian marble fireplaces and breathtaking surroundings.

LYNMAR ESTATE

Laguna de Santa Rosa, a twenty-two-mile sanctuary of creeks, wetlands, and oak woodlands, is the largest tributary of the Russian River. As Sonoma County's richest wildlife area, it supports river otters, western pond turtles, mountain lions, coyotes, steelhead trout, coho salmon, and more than two hundred species of birds. Lynmar Estate—a hundred-acre oasis with rolling hills, lush gardens, and native flowers and trees—borders the laguna, about twenty miles east of the Sonoma Coast.

Lynmar Estate's owners, Lynn Fritz and his wife, Anisya, bought the forty-eight-acre Quail Hill Ranch in 1980. They initially farmed the existing vineyards, planted in 1974, and sold the grapes to other winemakers. Fruit called Old Vines, was sold to (at Matanzas Creek at the time) fourteen years of witnessing Edwards and Soter were able to build a winery. Lynmar Estate  from a particular block, now winemakers Merry Edwards and Tony Soter at Etude. After the spectacular results that produce, the Fritzes decided to Winery released its inaugural 1994 vintage of Pinot Noirs and Chardonnays in 1996 and has used the Old Vines block as a key element of its wine program ever since.

Lynmar's estate Quail Hill Vineyard lies within one of the appellation's coolest areas, Laguna Ridge, an enviable microclimate for its primary grape varieties, Pinot Noir and Chardonnay. Lynmar also owns nearby Susanna's Vineyard, west of Quail Hill. Together, the vineyards have fourteen clones of Pinot Noir and five clones of Chardonnay, which provide winemaker Shane Finley with an expansive palette of flavors to craft acclaimed artisanal wines.

Lynmar's hospitality salon is reminiscent of an elegant residence. Visitors have multiple seating options: at the curved tasting bar or at various tables around the room and in adjacent alcoves, or in leather sofas and armchairs. A massive glass wall opens to the outdoor deck on fair-weather days. Set amid vineyards, both the tasting room and the nearby state-of-the-art gravity-flow winery with small stainless steel fermenters and magnificent caves were intended to blend into the surrounding landscape of the lush Russian River Valley. Lynmar Estate chef David Frakes, who joined the winery in 2011, refined his style of farm-to-table cuisine as executive chef at Applewood Inn in Guerneville and honed his expertise in pairing food with wine as executive chef at Beringer Vineyards. From May to October, he picks some of the estate-grown produce to create a seasonal picnic paired with limited-release Lynmar Estate wines, served on the tasting room courtyard overlooking the gardens, Quail Hill Vineyard, and the pristine Laguna de Santa Rosa.

LYNMAR ESTATE
3909 Frei Rd.
Sebastopol, CA 95472
707-829-3374
reserve@lynmarestate.com
lynmarestate.com

OWNERS:
Lynn and Anisya Fritz.

LOCATION: About 5 miles west of U.S. 101 via Guerneville Rd.

APPELLATION: Russian River Valley.

HOURS: 10 A.M.–4:30 P.M. daily, and by appointment.

TASTINGS: $15 for 4 wines; $25 for 4 reserve wines; $50 for hour-long hosted tasting of 6 limited-release wines paired with food, May–October, 11 A.M.– 2 P.M. Wednesday–Saturday, by appointment.

TOURS: None.

THE WINES: Chardonnay, Pinot Noir.

SPECIALTIES: Estate, vineyard-designated, and block-designated Pinot Noir.

WINEMAKER: Shane Finley.

ANNUAL PRODUCTION: 10,000 cases.

OF SPECIAL NOTE: Self-guided tour of extensive gardens. Seasonal bar menu offered daily year-round. Picnic pairings prepared by on-site chef mid-May through mid-October. Terrace courtyard with vineyard views. Most wines available only in tasting room.

NEARBY ATTRACTION: Laguna de Santa Rosa (freshwater wetlands with wildlife viewing).

MARTINELLI WINERY

MARTINELLI WINERY
3360 River Rd.
Windsor, CA 95492
800-346-1627
vinoinfo@
martinelliwinery.com
martinelliwinery.com

OWNERS: Lee Sr. and Carolyn Martinelli and their 4 children.

LOCATION: About 2 miles west of U.S. 101 via River Rd./Mark West Springs Rd. exit.

APPELLATIONS: Russian River Valley, Sonoma Coast, Fort Ross–Seaview, Green Valley of Russian River Valley.

HOURS: 10 A.M.–5 P.M. daily.

TASTINGS: $10.

TOURS: By appointment.

THE WINES: Chardonnay, Muscat Alexandria, Pinot Noir, Syrah, Zinfandel.

SPECIALTIES: Wines made from estate-grown grapes.

WINEMAKERS: Bryan Kvamme, winemaker; Erin Green, consulting winemaker.

ANNUAL PRODUCTION: 12,000 cases.

OF SPECIAL NOTE: All wines are made from estate grapes and are 100 percent varietal. Several picnic tables with vineyard views scattered throughout the property.

NEARBY ATTRACTIONS: Wells Fargo Center for the Performing Arts; Russian River (rafting, fishing, swimming, canoeing, kayaking).

The bright red hop barn sitting only a few yards off River Road is a photo opportunity waiting to happen. The tasting room entrance is a sheltered nook where wooden tables and benches, gracefully weathered to a soft gray, sit beneath a vine-covered trellis. Beyond the barn, rows of vineyards march up a hill, interspersed with a trio of arbors perfect for picnicking.

The scene could well be the setting for an old-fashioned movie romanticizing rural life, but the Martinelli Winery is the real thing. The Martinelli family has been growing grapes in the Russian River Valley since 1887, and successive generations have kept their immigrant ancestors' dreams alive over the decades.

At the tender ages of  nineteen and sixteen, Giuseppe Martinelli and Luisa Vellutini eloped from their village in the Tuscany region of Italy, bound for California in search of land where they could start a winery. Giuseppe had been a winemaker in Italy, and with his knowledge of viticulture, he was hired by a local farmer to work in a vineyard in Forestville. Within two years, the hardworking young man was able to purchase some land. Giuseppe and Luisa, working side by side on a sixty-degree slope, planted Zinfandel and Muscat Alexandria vines on what would eventually become known as the Jackass Hill vineyard. Luisa's uphill struggle was just beginning. Giuseppe died in 1918, leaving his widow with four children and a farm to run. The youngest Martinelli son, Leno, left school after the eighth grade and began farming the Zinfandel vineyard all by himself. How did the vineyard get its name? Leno's family told him that only a jackass would farm a hill that steep.

Armed with his parents' knowledge and his own experience, Leno persevered, even using a horse and plow to work the land until 1949, when he finally bought a tractor. Only at the age of eighty-nine did he finally hang up the keys to his John Deere and relinquish the reins to his son, Lee. In 1973 Lee took over management of his uncle Tony Bondi's adjacent estate, located minutes away from Jackass Hill, and planted vineyards where apple orchards once flourished.

When Lee and his wife, Carolyn, decided to start a winery on the property, they converted a pair of hop barns into the winemaking facility and tasting room, taking care to preserve the historic character of the buildings. Today, Lee Sr. and his two sons, Lee Jr. and George, do all the farming. References to the Martinelli farming heritage are visible in the cozy tasting room store, where, amid rustic hutches stocked with linens and unique gifts, ancient winery equipment and faded family photographs are on display.

MOSHIN VINEYARDS

Westside Road out of downtown Healdsburg follows the mild curves of the Russian River past vineyards of mostly Chardonnay and Pinot Noir grapes. About ten miles southwest of town, both road and river bend sharply, and a colorful, far-larger-than-life sculpture of a hummingbird drawing nectar from a flower hovers in midair, marking the short, secluded driveway that ends at the Moshin Vineyards tasting room. Fronted by weathered redwood reclaimed from the century-old barn of a neighboring property, the room and the winery behind it nuzzle into the surrounding hillside so comfortably that it may come as a surprise to learn both were completed in 2005.

The winery and the wines vision of Rick Moshin, a former for Pinot Noir wines is exceeded aspect of their creation. In this River Valley, it's not unheard of their tasting rooms to discuss made within it represent the math professor whose passion only by his attention to every placid portion of the Russian for winemakers to appear in their wines with visitors, but those lucky enough to stop here when Moshin is around might also hear him describe the intricacies of the energy-saving four-tier gravity-flow winery he designed, how he helped lay its foundation and build it, and how he milled and finished the sensually smooth tongue-and-groove black walnut tasting bar.

Sometimes a tasting bar is just a tasting bar, but in this case it provides clues about the artistry, precision, and scholarship that inform Moshin's lineup of a dozen-plus small-lot Pinot Noirs. They, along with Pinot Gris, Chardonnay, Zinfandel, and other wines, are made from grapes grown on twenty-eight estate acres and sourced from noted, mostly Sonoma County growers. Moshin, who started his winery in 1989, tends to pick Pinot Noir grapes on the early side to preserve the acidity, a European approach that often produces wines that pair well with food and age gracefully. They're also lower in alcohol than many of their Russian River counterparts.

Moshin's ultimate goal is to create affordable wines whose flavors—from the fruit, oak fermentation, tannins, and, most importantly, soil and climate—blend harmoniously. At tastings the choices include a few whites and, if available, a pale but zesty Rosé of Pinot Noir. The flavors of the Pinot Noirs range from the light and floral to bolder expressions of the varietal. The convivial, well-informed pourers share entertaining anecdotes about the wines, the winery, and the Russian River Valley appellation. The mood is so welcoming that in fine weather many guests extend their stay at the picnic tables near Rufus, the sculptural hummingbird, who's often joined by real ones flitting by.

MOSHIN VINEYARDS
10295 Westside Rd.
Healdsburg, CA 95448
707-433-5499
888-466-7446
moshin@moshinvineyards.com
moshinvineyards.com

OWNER: Rick Moshin.

LOCATION: 10 miles southwest of Healdsburg.

APPELLATION: Russian River Valley.

HOURS: 11 A.M.–4:30 P.M. daily.

TASTINGS: $10 for 5 wines (waived with purchase).

TOURS: By appointment ($20, includes tasting).

THE WINES: Chardonnay, Merlot, Pinot Noir, Sauvignon Blanc, Zinfandel.

SPECIALTIES: Small-lot vineyard-designated Pinot Noirs, Perpetual Moshin (Bordeaux blend), Moshin Potion No. 11 (white dessert wine).

WINEMAKER: Rick Moshin.

ANNUAL PRODUCTION: 9,000 cases.

OF SPECIAL NOTE: Russian River Valley's only four-tier gravity-flow winery. Picnic area. Art gallery with works by local and other Northern California artists. Events include quilting show (winter) and Barrel Tasting (March). Most wines available only in tasting room.

NEARBY ATTRACTIONS: Armstrong Redwoods State Natural Reserve (hiking, horseback riding); Russian River (rafting, fishing, swimming, canoeing, kayaking).

PAPAPIETRO PERRY

PAPAPIETRO PERRY
4791 Dry Creek Rd.
Healdsburg, CA 95448
877-GO-PINOT
707-433-0422
info@papapietro-perry
.com
papapietro-perry.com

OWNERS: Bruce and Renae
Perry, Ben and Yolanda
Papapietro.

LOCATION: 4.7 miles
northwest of Healdsburg.

APPELLATIONS: Anderson
Valley, Dry Creek Valley,
Russian River Valley,
Sonoma Coast.

HOURS: 11 A.M.–4:30 P.M.
daily.

TASTINGS: $10 for 5 wines.
Pinot on the Patio wine-
and-cheese tasting by
appointment.

TOURS: None.

THE WINES: Chardonnay,
Pinot Noir, Zinfandel.

SPECIALTY: Pinot Noir.

WINEMAKER:
Ben Papapietro.

ANNUAL PRODUCTION:
6,000–8,000 cases.

OF SPECIAL NOTE: Covered
patio with tables and views
of Dry Creek Valley; picnic
area; bocce ball. Annual
events include Winter
Wineland (January),
Barrel Tasting (March),
Passport to Dry Creek
Valley (April), Chardonnay
and Lobster (June), and
Wine and Food Affair
(November).

NEARBY ATTRACTIONS:
Lake Sonoma (hiking,
fishing, boating, camping,
swimming); Russian River
(swimming, canoeing,
kayaking, rafting, fishing);
Healdsburg Museum and
Historical Society; Hand
Fan Museum (collection
of antique fans).

A passion for Pinot Noir has connected Ben Papapietro and Bruce Perry for nearly forty years. Both grew up in San Francisco, in Italian and Portuguese families who always served wine at meals and gatherings. Their grandfathers made wine at home in the basement, and the young boys watched and listened, learning the basic techniques of the craft. They also developed a keen, lifelong interest in cooking and wine.

As a young man, Ben Papapietro sampled various Burgundian wines and fell in love with Pinot Noir. Purchasing this varietal for daily consumption, however, would certainly break the family bank. So he began making his own wines at home in the garage, following his ancestral traditions. In the 1970s, while working at the San Francisco Newspaper Agency, he became friends with Bruce Perry, who sampled and liked Papapietro's garage-made wines and joined in on the endeavor. After producing several varietals, they knew it was Pinot Noir that won their hearts. Burt Williams, who worked at the San Francisco Newspaper Agency, was also an avid home winemaker. In the early 1980s, Williams cofounded Williams Selyem, a Sonoma winery famed for its Pinot Noir production. Ben and Bruce worked there during annual harvests and honed their winemaking skills.

More than a decade later, the two friends felt ready to introduce their Pinot Noir to the public. They located a winemaking facility in Sonoma County and founded Papapietro Perry Winery in 1998. Bruce and Ben eventually left their day jobs and dove full force into the business, with Bruce and Ben making the wine and Bruce's wife, Renae, running the business. Later, Ben's wife, Yolanda, joined to handle distributor relations.

The devoted attention paid off quickly, as Papapietro Perry wines have consistently earned high praise and awards from critics since the early 2000s. Ben Papapietro's winemaking skills have also garnered acclaim among Pinot Noir devotees. Today the winery produces ten Pinot Noirs and a small amount of Zinfandel and Chardonnay. Grapes come from established vineyards in the Russian River Valley, as well as surrounding Dry Creek Valley, Anderson Valley, and the Sonoma Coast.

The Papapietro Perry tasting room opened in 2005 at Timber Crest Farms, in the heart of pastoral Dry Creek Valley. The former farm now houses a collection of wineries and other small businesses. Visitors taste wines at a gleaming copper-topped bar made of intricately woven barrel staves, which Bruce Perry built by hand. In many ways, the unpretentious space reflects the winery's homey, but humble beginnings in the family garage more than three decades past.

PATZ & HALL

PATZ & HALL
21200 8th St. East
Sonoma, CA 95476
707-265-7700
info@patzhall.com
patzhall.com

OWNERS: Donald Patz,
James Hall, Anne Moses,
Heather Patz.

LOCATION: 3 miles southeast
of historic Sonoma Plaza.

APPELLATIONS: Sonoma
Valley, Sonoma Coast,
Green Valley of Russian
River Valley, Los Carneros,
Russian River Valley,
Mendocino.

HOURS: 10 A.M.–4 P.M.
Thursday–Monday

TASTINGS: $25 for 4 wines,
held on the hour; $40 for
Terrace Tasting of 4 single-
vineyard wines paired with
food, by appointment;
$50 for Salon tasting of 6
reserve wines paired with
food, by appointment.

TOURS: None.

THE WINES: Chardonnay,
Pinot Noir, sparkling wine.

SPECIALTIES: Vineyard-
designated Chardonnay
and Pinot Noir.

WINEMAKER: James Hall.

ANNUAL PRODUCTION:
28,000 cases.

OF SPECIAL NOTE: Vineyard-
view patio with seating,
fountain, and large lawn
with games. Gifts, jewelry,
and wine-themed items
available for purchase.
Featured visual artist each
quarter. Outdoor events
monthly June–September.
Annual events include
Spring Release Open House
(two Saturdays in March)
and Fall Release Party (first
Saturday in October). Many
wines available only in tasting room.

NEARBY ATTRACTIONS:
Historic buildings in down-
town Sonoma; bike rentals;
Vella Cheese Company.

Sonoma House, the gleaming new Patz & Hall hospitality center, sits amid lush vineyards in the rural east side of the town of Sonoma. For nearly a decade, the winery tasting room had been located in a modest office building near the city of Napa. When sixteen acres with a single-family residence became available up the road from its Sonoma winemaking facility, Patz & Hall seized the opportunity to transform the estate property into a one-of-a-kind wine country complex. The goal was to have a number of indoor and outdoor areas where the winery could welcome customers and get to know them in person. Sonoma House opened to the public in early 2014 following an extensive remodel that pre-  served the feel of a family home while adding contemporary flair and furnishings.

Patz & Hall was estab- lished in 1988 by four indivi- duals — Donald Patz, James Hall, Anne Moses, and Heather Patz — who dedicated them- selves to making benchmark wines sourced from distinctive California vineyards. Today, they produce a total of fifteen Chardonnays and Pinot Noirs, all without owning a single vineyard themselves. Patz & Hall was founded on an unusual business model that began in the 1980s at Flora Springs Winery & Vineyards, when assistant winemaker James Hall and national sales manager Donald Patz forged a close friendship. Their mutual enthu- siasm for wine produced from elite, small vineyards inspired them to blend their talents along with those of Anne Moses and Heather Patz. Together, the team boasted a wealth of knowledge and ex- perience gleaned at such prestigious Northern California wineries as Far Niente, Girard Winery, and Honig Winery, where Hall was once the winemaker.

The founders applied their specialized expertise and daily attention to different areas of the family-run winery's operations. The cornerstone of Patz & Hall is this integrated, hands-on approach, combined with close personal relationships with growers who supply them with fruit from outstanding family-owned vineyards.

Visitors to Sonoma House can sit on leather stools at the marble tasting bar, where casual tasting takes place, or can join a private, hour-long tasting, paired with food, in the elegant Sonoma House Salon. Guided tastings are also held on the shaded outdoor terrace. Over the course of an hour or more, guests sample single-vineyard wines paired with local farmstead cheeses and other light fare. Visitors are welcome to sink into comfortable sofas and chairs by a roaring fire in the living room in winter, or in fair weather in oversized rattan chairs on the terrace or back lawns, where they enjoy stunning views of the Mayacamas Mountains and estate vineyards.

RAVENSWOOD WINERY

RAVENSWOOD WINERY
18701 Gehricke Rd.
Sonoma, CA 95476
707-933-2332
888-669-4679
ravenswoodwinery. com

OWNER:
Constellation Brands.

LOCATION: About .5 mile
northeast of the town of
Sonoma via Fourth St.
East and Lovall Valley Rd.

APPELLATION:
Sonoma Valley.

HOURS: 10 A.M.–4:30 P.M.
daily.

TASTINGS: $15 for vineyard-
designated wines.

TOURS: 10:30 A.M. daily
($20).

THE WINES: Bordeaux-style
blends, Cabernet Franc,
Cabernet Sauvignon,
Chardonnay, Icon
(Zinfandel, Carignane,
Petite Sirah, Alicante
Bouschet), Muscato, Petite
Sirah, Zinfandel.

SPECIALTY: Zinfandel.

WINEMAKER: Joel Peterson.

ANNUAL PRODUCTION:
500,000 cases.

OF SPECIAL NOTE: Blending
seminars by appointment.
Bicyclists and other
visitors are welcome to
picnic on stone patio with
view of vineyards.

NEARBY ATTRACTIONS:
Mission San Francisco
Solano, Lachryma Montis
(Mariano Vallejo's
estate), and other historic
buildings in downtown
Sonoma; bike rentals; Vella
Cheese Company; Sonoma
Cheese Factory; Sonoma
Traintown (rides on a scale
railroad).

ew wineries set out to make cult wines, and probably fewer earn a widespread following as well. Ravenswood has done both. Its founders began by crushing enough juice to produce 327 cases of Zinfandel in 1976, and although the winery also makes other wines, Zinfandel remains king. Nearly three-quarters of Ravenswood's production is Zinfandel.

Winemaker and cofounder Joel Peterson and chairman and cofounder Reed Foster were so successful with that first, handcrafted vintage that they have had to live up to the standard it set ever since. Ravenswood produces fourteen different Zinfandels that represent the spectrum of the varietal's personality, with tastes ranging from peppery and spicy to chocolaty and minty. If there is one common denominator, it is reflected in the slogan adopted by the winery in 1990: "No Wimpy Wines."

Most of Ravenswood's grapes come from more than a hundred independent growers. It is those long-standing relationships that ensure the consistency of the wines. One vineyard source dates to 1886. The Strotz family invited Joel Peterson to visit their Sonoma Mountain vineyard, which they had named Pickberry because of all the wild blackberries harvested there. Peterson immediately recognized the quality of the Strotz grapes, and in 1988 Ravenswood released the first of its many blends of Cabernet Sauvignon, Cabernet Franc, and Merlot under the vineyard-designated name Pickberry.

Peterson never set out to specialize in Zinfandel; originally he was more interested in the Bordeaux varietals he began tasting at the age of ten with his father, Walter, founder of the San Francisco Wine Sampling Club. In time, however, he fell under the spell of Zinfandel. In the 1970s, after a brief career as a wine writer and consultant, he went to work for the late Joseph Swan, considered one of California's outstanding craftsmen of fine Zinfandel. Thus the stage was set for the varietal's ascendancy at the winery Peterson founded.

Ravenswood farms fourteen acres of estate vineyards on the northeast side of Sonoma. The old stone building, once home to the Haywood Winery, has extensive patio seating with beautiful south-facing views of the vineyards. Thanks to the company's growth, the winemaking operations have since been relocated to a 45,000-square-foot facility in Carneros, to the south, but the tasting room remains. Originally a cozy, even cramped affair, it was greatly expanded in 1996, and now has plenty of elbow room as well as ample natural light for visitors who come to sample and appreciate the wines.

TASTING ROOM
OPEN FROM 10-4:30

NO
BUSES
PLEASE

PARKING

RODNEY STRONG VINEYARDS

In the 1940s Rodney D. Strong trained with dance masters Martha Graham and George Balanchine at the American School of Ballet in New York. He enjoyed a successful career in the United States and abroad, including a four-year stint in Paris, where he developed a passion for food and fine wine. In 1959 Strong retired from dance, married his dance partner Charlotte Ann Winson, and planned to start a career in winemaking. The couple moved to Northern California, purchased a century-old boarding house in Windsor, and began making their first wines.

As Strong perfected his winemaking skills, he proved to have an innate ability to see the potential of undiscovered growing regions. In 1962 he bought a turn-of-the-century winery and 159-acre vineyard in Windsor 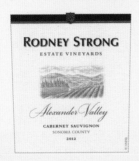 and replanted the vineyard to Chardonnay vines—the first in what later became the celebrated Chalk Hill AVA. In 1968, using U.C. Davis climate data as a guide, Strong purchased land in the Russian River Valley and planted several of the region's first Pinot Noir vineyards. He also built an impressive, efficient winery building, completed in 1970. Six years later, Rodney Strong Vineyards introduced Alexander's Crown, Sonoma County's first single-vineyard Cabernet Sauvignon. In 1977 the winery released the first Chardonnay bearing the Chalk Hill designation.

A decade later, as Strong was ready to transition into retirement, business consultant Tom Klein wanted to invest in the wine industry and recognized the untapped potential of Rodney Strong Vineyards. He convinced his family to purchase the winery in 1989. Over the decades, they installed state-of-the-art facilities, including a temperature-controlled barrel house and two artisan cellars for crafting small lots of wine. The family also took steps to reduce the winery's carbon footprint, and in 2009 Rodney Strong Vineyards became the first carbon-neutral winery in Sonoma County. Today it owns thirteen estate vineyards in six appellations, providing winemaker Rick Sayre, head winemaker since 1979, with a vast selection of varietals for crafting four tiers of wines: single vineyard, reserve, estate, and Sonoma County.

The original 1970 winery building continues to serve as the hospitality center, where visitors sample wines at a semicircular, granite-topped bar and at redwood-barrel tables. Exhibits on winemaking techniques and Sonoma County viticulture history are mounted along an open walkway and decks that surround the tasting room. On fair-weather days, seated food-and-wine pairings are held on the winery's canopy-shaded terrace, a new feature added in 2014, which is ringed with Chinese pistache trees.

RODNEY STRONG VINEYARDS
11455 Old Redwood Hwy.
Healdsburg, CA 95448
800-678-4763
info@rodneystrong.com
rodneystrong.com

OWNER: Tom Klein.

LOCATION: 3 miles south of Healdsburg via Old Redwood Hwy. exit off U.S. 101.

APPELLATIONS: Alexander Valley, Chalk Hill, Dry Creek Valley, Northern Sonoma, Russian River Valley, Sonoma Coast.

HOURS: 10 A.M.–5 P.M. daily.

TASTINGS: Complimentary for 2 wines; $10 for 4 estate wines; $15 for reserve tasting of 4 single-vineyard wines.

TOURS: Free guided tour at 11 A.M. and 3 P.M. daily. Self-guided tour 10 A.M.–5 P.M. daily

THE WINES: Cabernet Sauvignon, Chardonnay, Merlot, Pinot Noir, Sauvignon Blanc, Symmetry (red Meritage Bordeaux blend), Syrah, Zinfandel.

SPECIALTY: Sonoma County vineyard-designated Cabernet Sauvignon.

WINEMAKER: Rick Sayre.

ANNUAL PRODUCTION: Unavailable.

OF SPECIAL NOTE: Summer outdoor concert series. Picnic area with tables on lawns overlooking vineyards. Extensive gift shop. Bar menu available in tasting room. Annual events include Winter Wineland (January), Barrel Tasting (March), Passport to Dry Creek Valley (April), and Wine and Food Affair (November).

NEARBY ATTRACTIONS: Russian River (swimming, canoeing, kayaking, rafting, fishing); Healdsburg Museum and Historical Society (changing exhibits about Sonoma County).

THREE STICKS WINES

THREE STICKS WINES
143 W. Spain St.
Sonoma, CA 95476
707-996-3328, ext. 105
info@threestickswines.com
threestickswines.com

OWNERS: Bill and Eva Price.

LOCATION: Half block west of Sonoma Plaza's northwest corner.

APPELLATIONS: Sonoma Valley, Sonoma Coast, Sonoma Mountain, Moon Mountain District, Russian River Valley.

HOURS: 11 A.M.–5 P.M. Monday–Saturday, by appointment only.

TASTINGS: $35 for 4 current release wines, $70 for 7 library and current release wines.

TOURS: Guided tours of historic Vallejo-Casteñada Adobe included with tasting. Vineyard tours available seasonally.

THE WINES: Cabernet Sauvignon, Chardonnay, Pinot Noir.

SPECIALTIES: Small-lot, single-vineyard Chardonnays and Pinot Noirs.

WINEMAKER: Don Van Staaveren.

ANNUAL PRODUCTION: 5,000 cases.

OF SPECIAL NOTE: The adobe is the oldest occupied residence in Sonoma. Original garden designed by landscape architect Helen Van Pelt in 1948 and redesigned by Penney Magrane in 2013. Casteñada Rhône blend available only at winery.

NEARBY ATTRACTIONS: Mission San Francisco Solano, Lachryma Montis (Mariano Vallejo's estate), and other historic buildings in downtown Sonoma; bike rentals; Vella Cheese Company; Sonoma Cheese Factory; Sonoma Traintown (rides on a scale railroad).

After a dazzling restoration, one of Sonoma's oldest adobes from California's period of Mexican rule (1822–1846) reopened in 2014 as the tasting salon of Three Sticks Wines. The makeover's first phase involved a historically sensitive retrofitting of the entire structure. That task completed, owner Bill Price brought in Ken Fulk, a San Francisco–based tastemaker and celebrity designer, who created an understatedly exuberant interior space that evokes the Mexican period through its textures and earth tones, yet feels emphatically au courant.

The Vallejo-Casteñada Adobe, built in 1842, takes its name from the surnames of its original owner, Salvador Vallejo, and occupant, Don Juan Casteñada. At the time, Salvador's brother, Mariano

Vallejo, was Mexico's highest-ranking military commander in the northern frontier of Alta California, and Don Juan served as Mariano's secretary. California's declaration of independence from Mexico took place in Sonoma Plaza in 1846, mere steps from the adobe, and a decade later Count Agoston Haraszthy ushered in the modern era of California winemaking when he opened the Buena Vista Winery a few miles away.

Sonoma's rich history and the adobe's are among the topics discussed at hosted, seated tastings limited to eight participants. The exclusive sessions include a tour of the adobe and its garden, where vegetation planted by previous owners, augmented by recent additions, provides a lush backdrop for contemporary elements — fountains, a fire pit, and two arbors fashioned of willow branches supported by thick reclaimed Douglas fir beams. Depending on the weather and guests' preferences, tastings unfold either inside the adobe at a handcrafted elm table or outside in the garden at a cast stone table that rests atop 140-year-old barn beams.

While Price was a principal in an investment company with major wine holdings that included Chateau St. Jean in Kenwood, he developed a passion for Pinot Noir that eventually inspired the creation of Three Sticks. To create a wine program built around that varietal and Chardonnay and Cabernet Sauvignon, Price enlisted Don Van Staaveren as winemaker. Van Staaveren raised Chateau St. Jean's profile — and arguably the entire Sonoma Valley's — with a 1996 Cabernet Sauvignon blend that *Wine Spectator* named Wine of the Year, the first ever from Sonoma County. One might assume the origins of Price's winery's name are grape related, but they actually derive from his high school days in Hawaii as a surfer. His fellow surfers (who these days include Van Staaveren) dubbed him "Billy Three Sticks," after the Roman numerals in his full name, Bill Price III.

WALT WINES

A canary palm towers over the cream-colored Tudor-style home that serves as the Walt Wines tasting room just off the historic Sonoma Plaza. Built during the Depression for an employee of the Sebastianis, one of Sonoma's oldest wine families, the home, trimmed in forest green, now hosts this relative newcomer that specializes in small-lot, single-vineyard Pinot Noirs. A sister winery to Hall St. Helena in the Napa Valley, Walt was named by proprietor Kathryn Walt Hall to honor her parents, Dolores and Bob Walt, longtime Mendocino County grape growers she credits with inspiring her passion for winemaking.

The handsome Walt logo incorporates interlocking bands of color representing the four primary Pinot Noir growing sources its grapes: Oregon's County's Anderson Valley, Coast and Russian River appel- of California's Central Coast. Walt provides Pinot aficiona- ience how one winemaker— with input from Steve Leveque,

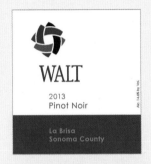

regions from which the winery Willamette Valley, Mendocino Sonoma County's Sonoma lations, and the Santa Rita Hills With a portfolio this diverse, dos the opportunity to exper- in this case Megan Gunderson, director of winemaking for Hall and Walt—crafts wines from distinct grape clones grown in different climates and soils.

Gunderson's previous positions before Hall (where she serves as Leveque's assistant winemaker) and Walt include the Robert Mondavi, St. Supéry, and Dominus Estate wineries in the Napa Valley. Drawing on her experiences at these facilities and her background in biochemistry and molecular genetics, she strives to make each wine express its particular vineyard and region. To achieve this goal, Gunderson implements both contemporary and traditional winemaking techniques. Grapes are harvested at night, for instance, when the cooler temperatures yield lower sugar levels, a fairly recent practice whose benefits include a more stable fermentation process. In a bow to old-world winemaking, the grapes are all hand sorted, native rather than commercial yeasts are utilized during fermentation, and the wines are neither filtered nor fined to make them appear clearer.

The tasting room's congenial staff is well versed in the regional nuances of the Walt Pinot Noirs and the winery's minimalistic approach. Tastings generally begin with a Chardonnay, followed by four Pinot Noirs, poured in the original occupants' living and dining rooms. The domestic ambience encourages lingering, as do the curated art shows, usually of paintings or photography. If the weather's fine, tastings also take place on three redwood picnic tables on the gravel patio out back, where a substantial doubled-stemmed redwood tree provides ample shade.

WALT WINES
380 1st St. West
Sonoma, CA 95476
707-933-4440
info@waltwines.com
waltwines.com

OWNERS: Kathryn Walt Hall and Craig Hall.

LOCATION: Just north of northwest corner of Sonoma Plaza.

APPELLATIONS: Sonoma Coast, Russian River Valley, Anderson Valley (Mendocino), Sta. Rita Hills (Central Coast), Willamette Valley (Oregon).

HOURS: 11 A.M.–6 P.M. daily.

TASTINGS: $20 for 5 wines.

TOURS: None.

THE WINES: Chardonnay, Pinot Noir.

SPECIALTY: Single-vineyard Pinot Noir.

WINEMAKER: Megan Gunderson.

ANNUAL PRODUCTION: 10,000 cases.

OF SPECIAL NOTE: Tastings held on outdoor patio in good weather. Contemporary art on display. Food-and-wine pairings by appointment. Pinot Noirs available only in tasting room.

NEARBY ATTRACTIONS: Mission San Francisco Solano, Lachryma Montis (Mariano Vallejo's estate), and other historic buildings in downtown Sonoma; bike rentals; Vella Cheese Company; Sonoma Cheese Factory; Sonoma Traintown (rides on a scale railroad).

MENDOCINO

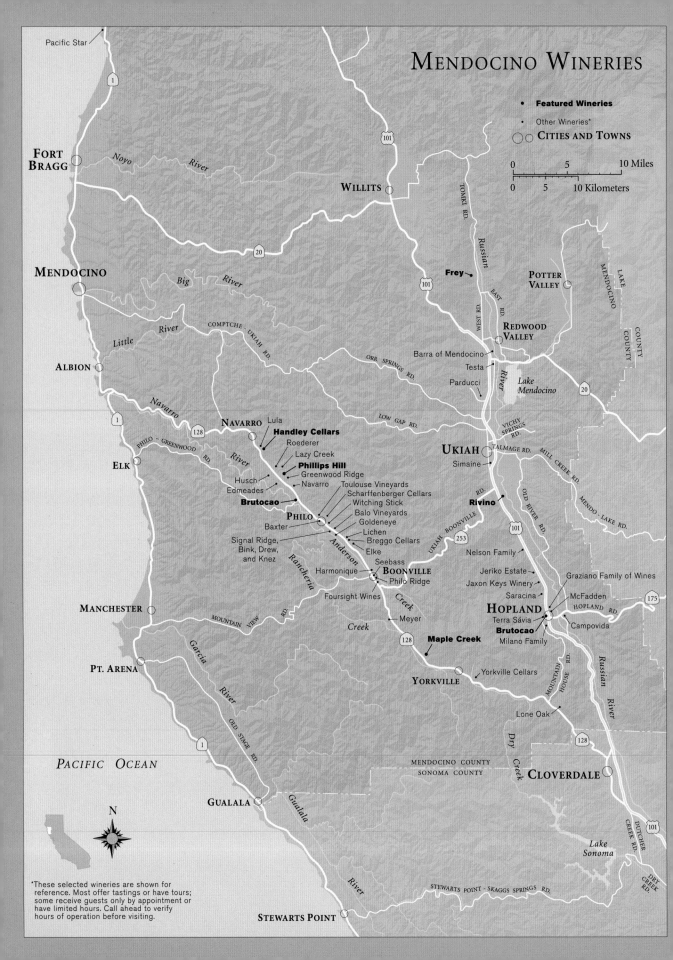

MENDOCINO WINERIES

- ● **Featured Wineries**
- • Other Wineries*
- ○ ⬭ **CITIES AND TOWNS**

0 — 5 — 10 Miles
0 — 5 — 10 Kilometers

Pacific Star

FORT BRAGG

Noyo River

WILLITS

MENDOCINO

Big River

Frey

POTTER VALLEY

REDWOOD VALLEY

Barra of Mendocino
Testa
Parducci

Lake Mendocino

Comptche River

Little River

ALBION

COMPTCHE - UKIAH RD.

ORR SPRINGS RD.

LOW GAP RD.

TOMKI RD.
Russian
EAST RD.
WEST RD.

VICHY SPRINGS RD.

UKIAH
Simaine

TALMAGE RD.
MILL CREEK RD.
MENDO - LAKE RD.

Navarro River

NAVARRO   Lula
Handley Cellars
Roederer
Lazy Creek
Phillips Hill
Greenwood Ridge
Navarro
Husch
Edmeades
Brutocao

ELK

PHILO - GREENWOOD RD.

Toulouse Vineyards
Scharffenberger Cellars
Witching Stick
Balo Vineyards
Goldeneye
Lichen
Breggo Cellars
Elke
Seebass

PHILO
Baxter
Signal Ridge,
Bink, Drew,
and Knez

Harmonique

Anderson

Rivino

UKIAH BOONVILLE RD.
253
OLD RIVER RD.
101

Nelson Family

BOONVILLE
Philo Ridge

Foursight Wines

Rancheria

Creek

Meyer

Creek

Jeriko Estate
Jaxon Keys Winery
Saracina

Graziano Family of Wines
McFadden

HOPLAND
Terra Sávia
Brutocao
Milano Family

Campovida

HOPLAND RD.
175

MOUNTAIN VIEW RD.

128
Maple Creek

MANCHESTER

Garcia River

PT. ARENA

OLD STAGE RD.

YORKVILLE
Yorkville Cellars

Lone Oak

MOUNTAIN HOUSE RD.

Russian River

128

Dry Creek

Lake Sonoma

PACIFIC OCEAN

N

MENDOCINO COUNTY
SONOMA COUNTY

CLOVERDALE

101

DUTCHER CREEK RD.

DRY CREEK RD.

GUALALA

Gualala River

*These selected wineries are shown for
reference. Most offer tastings or have tours;
some receive guests only by appointment or
have limited hours. Call ahead to verify
hours of operation before visiting.

STEWARTS POINT - SKAGGS SPRINGS RD.

STEWARTS POINT

River

Mendocino's dramatic coastline has made it famous all over the world, but the county offers a lot more than ocean views and rustic coastal inns. Now inland Mendocino is getting its due, thanks to local winemakers who are proving that their grapes are on a par with those of nearby Sonoma and Napa.

Vineyards were first planted here in the 1850s, when immigrants began farming food crops on the river plains and vineyards on the rugged hillsides and sun-exposed ridgetops. In time, they and their  successors found fertile ground in cooler areas that led them to achieve great success with a wide spec- trum of grape varieties.

Located too far north to transport their wines to the San Francisco market by boat—as Napa and Sonoma winemakers could—Mendocino's early grape growers sold and traded their crops closer to home. In the 1960s, the wine boom and advances in shipping brought Mendocino wines to markets farther afield. Today, the county boasts ninety-three wineries, so many of them involving organic wines or vineyards that the county bills itself as "America's Greenest Wine Region."

Mendocino's pioneer spirit still flourishes and is reflected in a serious respect for the environment. Most of the county is an undeveloped, pristine landscape offering abundant opportunities for enjoying an enviable variety of outdoor pursuits.

BRUTOCAO FAMILY VINEYARDS

Brutocao Family Vineyards is a tale of two families who combined their skills and expertise to establish one of Mendocino County's most notable wineries. The Brutocaos immigrated from Venice in the early 1900s, bringing with them a passion for wine. Len Brutocao met Marty Bliss while in school at Berkeley. Marty's father, Irv, had been farming land in Mendocino since the 1940s. Len and Marty married, and soon thereafter the families joined forces and began to grow grapes. The family sold their grapes to other wineries for years before starting

to make their own wine in 1991. They selected the Lion of St. Mark from St. Mark's Cathedral in Venice as their symbol of family tradition and quality. The heart of that quality, they say, is in their 575 acres of vineyards in southern Mendocino County and another 11 acres of Pinot Noir in Anderson Valley.

Today, four generations of Brutocaos continue the family traditions, using estate grapes to produce a wide range of wines, including Italian varietals and blends. The wines are bottled under two labels: Brutocao Cellars, which focuses on premium vintages, and Bliss Family Vineyards, a new line of reasonably priced wines. The winery's first tasting room, a redwood building once occupied by another winery, is in Anderson Valley, site of the Brutocao family's eleven-acre cool-climate Pinot Noir vineyard. With its high-beamed ceilings, wisteria-covered patio, and umbrella-shaded picnic tables, it makes an ideal stop for those traveling scenic Highway 128 to the Pacific Coast.

In the late 1990s, the Brutocaos decided to open a second tasting room on U.S. 101. In 1997 they purchased the old Hopland High School from the Fetzer wine family and created a seven-and-a-half-acre complex, Schoolhouse Plaza, dedicated to food and wine. Both a tasting room and a banquet area with full kitchen are in the remodeled 1920s building, which still has its original facade bearing the high school's name. On display in the tasting room are memorabilia from the school's glory days. The complex also has a large conference room and an antique bar. Visitors can sip a glass of wine while perusing the large gift shop or overlooking the landscaped grounds, which include beautiful gardens of lavender, roses, and wildflowers.

The Brutocaos brought more than a love of food and wine when they came to this country. They are also passionate about bocce ball, a devilishly challenging game with a half-century Italian lineage. The Hopland complex has six regulation bocce ball courts, which are lighted and open to the public. Visitors can participate in friendly competitions free of charge or watch the games as they relax on terraces or the expanse of manicured lawn with a peaked-roof gazebo.

BRUTOCAO FAMILY VINEYARDS ANDERSON VALLEY TASTING ROOM:
7000 Hwy. 128
Philo, CA 95466
800-661-2103
SCHOOLHOUSE PLAZA:
13500 U.S. 101
Hopland, CA 95449
800-433-3689
brutocao@pacific.net
brutocaocellars.com

OWNERS: Brutocao family.

LOCATIONS: Hwy. 128 in Anderson Valley; U.S. 101 in downtown Hopland.

APPELLATIONS: Anderson Valley, Mendocino.

HOURS: 10 A.M.–5 P.M. daily (both locations).

TASTINGS: Complimentary.

TOURS: By appointment (complimentary).

THE WINES: Barbera, Cabernet Sauvignon, Chardonnay, Dolcetto, Merlot, Pinot Noir, Port, Primitivo, Sangiovese, Sauvignon Blanc, Zinfandel.

SPECIALTIES: Italian varietals, Quadriga (Italian varietal blend).

WINEMAKER: Hoss Milone.

ANNUAL PRODUCTION: 15,000 cases.

OF SPECIAL NOTE: Hopland: Bocce courts. New on-site restaurant. Picnic areas with tables on shaded terraces. Annual events include Hopland Passport (May and October). Philo: Picnic area with tables and umbrellas under a shade arbor. Annual events include Anderson Valley Pinot Noir Festival (May). Port and reserve wines available only in tasting rooms.

NEARBY ATTRACTIONS: Hopland: Real Goods Solar Living Center (tours, store). Philo: Hendy Woods State Park (hiking, camping).

FREY VINEYARDS, LTD.

FREY VINEYARDS, LTD.
14000 Tomki Rd.
Redwood Valley, CA 95470
707-485-5177
800-760-3739
info@freywine.com
freywine.com

OWNERS: Frey family.

LOCATION: 15 miles north of Ukiah off U.S. 101.

APPELLATION: Redwood Valley.

HOURS: By appointment.

TASTINGS: Complimentary.

TOURS: By appointment.

THE WINES: Cabernet Sauvignon, Chardonnay, Gewürztraminer, Merlot, Petite Sirah, Pinot Noir, Sangiovese, Sauvignon Blanc, Syrah, Zinfandel.

SPECIALTIES: Certified organic wines without added sulfites; biodynamic estate-bottled wines.

WINEMAKERS: Paul Frey and Jonathan Frey.

ANNUAL PRODUCTION: 125,000 cases.

OF SPECIAL NOTE: Picnic area for visitors' use. First American winery to receive Demeter biodynamic certification.

NEARBY ATTRACTIONS: Real Goods Solar Living Center (tours, store); Lake Mendocino (hiking, boating, fishing, camping); Grace Hudson Museum (Pomo Indian baskets, historical photographs, changing art exhibits); Orr Hot Springs (mineral springs spa).

rguably the most low-key winery in California, this gem is hidden off a two-lane road that wends through an undeveloped corner of Redwood Valley. Unsuspecting visitors might mistake the first building for the tasting room, but that's grandma's house. They must drive past it to reach the winery, and upon arriving, they find that there is no formal tasting room. Instead, tastings are conducted outdoors at a couple of planks set over a pair of wine barrels. When temperatures drop or rain falls, everyone retires to the original house—a redwood structure fashioned from an old barn—where the senior Mrs. Frey lives. Visitors are encouraged to picnic at one of several redwood tables

and benches hand-hewn by the late family patriarch, Paul.

Virtually everything at this winery seems handmade or fashioned from something else. Barrels and tanks have been salvaged from larger operations, and the winery itself was constructed of redwood from a defunct winery in Ukiah. Some rows of grapevines are interplanted with heirloom grains, which are harvested and ground into flour.

Frey (pronounced "fry") Vineyards is the oldest and largest all-organic winery in the United States. It may have another claim to fame as the winery with the most family members on the payroll. In 1961 Paul and Marguerite Frey, both doctors, bought ninety-nine acres near the headwaters of the Russian River. The Redwood Valley property seemed a great place to raise a family. Five of the couple's twelve children were born after the move, and most are still in the neighborhood.

In 1965 the Freys planted forty acres of Cabernet Sauvignon and Gray Riesling grapevines on the ranch's old pastureland, but they didn't start making wine until the 1970s. Eldest son Jonathan, who studied organic viticulture, began tending the vineyards and harvesting the grapes, which at first were sold to other wineries. When a Cabernet Sauvignon made with their grapes won a gold medal for a Santa Cruz winery, the family realized the vineyard's potential. Frey Vineyards was founded the next year, in 1980.

In 1996 the family began farming biodynamically. The word *biodynamic* stems from the agricultural theories of Austrian scientist and educator Rudolf Steiner. Biodynamic practices undertake to restore vitality to the soil. The farm is managed as a self-sustaining ecosystem, using special composting methods and specific planting times. As good stewards of the land, Frey started the first organic winery and was the first American winery fully certified by Demeter, the biodynamic certification organization. The wines have won many gold and silver medals for excellence.

HANDLEY CELLARS

As the crow flies, Anderson Valley's "deep end"—the far western reaches of the AVA—lies just ten miles from the Pacific Coast. It's one of California's coolest grape-growing regions, where cool foggy nights and bright sunny days prevail, ideal conditions for Pinot Noir, Chardonnay, and Gewürztraminer cultivation. Handley Cellars occupies nearly sixty acres in the northwest corner of this pastoral region, accessible from east or west via scenic Highway 128. The estate was once part of the historic Holmes Ranch and still includes the original ranch house, barn, and water tower, built in 1908.

Owner and winemaker Milla Handley grew up in the Bay Area with cosmopolitan parents who made wine a regular part of the family meals. She earned a degree in fermentation science from U.C. Davis in 1975 and  refined her craft working for winemakers Richard Arrowood at Chateau St. Jean and Jed Steele at Edmeades. In the early 1980s, eager to produce wine that reflected what she deemed the "essence" of Anderson Valley, Handley bought property at the Holmes Ranch. She planted her estate vineyard in 1982, built the winery three years later, and in 1987 opened the tasting room.

Handley shows her deep commitment to environmental stewardship in various ways. She farms responsibly, using organic methods and avoiding chemicals whenever possible. Behind the crush pad, she erected a solar array, which supplies 75 percent of the winery's energy. In 2013 she installed a complimentary electric vehicle charging station for environmentally conscious guests. To supplement the fruit grown in her thirty-acre vineyard—certified organic in 2005—Handley planted eight more acres at her home on the ridge above the winery. She also buys grapes from vineyards throughout Mendocino County, most from small family growers who share the same commitment to organic and sustainable farming. Handley crafts wines known for their distinctive character and balance, and ability to pair well with diverse international cuisines.

Handley Cellars rewards visitors with sweeping views of vineyard-stitched hills and ridgelines bristling with redwood trees—best enjoyed from shaded tables and Adirondack chairs in the new picnic area on the front lawn, completed in the summer of 2014. Indoors, the winery offers relaxed tastings amid a veritable gallery of antiques and folk art. When Handley was a child, her parents traveled to India, igniting a lifetime passion for collecting international folk art. Framed swatches of African Kuba cloth bear the angular patterns that inspired the winery's label art. In the adjacent courtyard garden, picnickers can enjoy a glass of wine while admiring exotic sculptures.

HANDLEY CELLARS
3151 Hwy. 128
Philo, CA 95466
707-895-3876
800-733-3151
info@handleycellars.com
handleycellars.com

OWNER: Milla Handley.

LOCATION: 6 miles northwest of Philo, 10 miles from Mendocino Coast.

APPELLATIONS: Anderson Valley, Mendocino.

HOURS: 10 A.M.–6 P.M. daily in summer, 10 A.M.–5 P.M. daily in winter.

TASTINGS: Complimentary for 5–9 wines; $15 for 5 reserve wines paired with cheeses and estate products such as olives and Pinot Noir onion jam.

TOURS: By appointment.

THE WINES: Chardonnay, Gewürztraminer, Pinot Gris, Pinot Noir, Riesling, Sauvignon Blanc, Syrah, Viognier, Zinfandel.

SPECIALTIES: Estate Chardonnay, Pinot Noir, sparkling wine.

WINEMAKERS: Milla Handley and Randy Schock.

ANNUAL PRODUCTION: 10,000 cases.

OF SPECIAL NOTE: New picnic area. Complimentary food-and-wine pairings the first weekend of each month. Art in the Cellar event held first week of February. Locally made jewelry and international folk art and crafts for sale in tasting room. Electric vehicle charging station free for guests. Events include Anderson Valley Barrel Tasting Weekend (July). Proprietary blends, sparkling wine, and late-harvest wines available only in tasting room.

NEARBY ATTRACTION: Hendy Woods State Park (hiking, camping).

MAPLE CREEK WINERY

MAPLE CREEK WINERY
20799 Hwy. 128
Yorkville, CA 95494
707-895-3001
tom@maplecreekwine.com
maplecreekwine.com

OWNER: Tom Rodrigues.

LOCATION: 20 miles northwest of Cloverdale.

APPELLATION: Yorkville Highlands.

HOURS: 11 A.M.–5 P.M. daily.

TASTINGS: $5 for minimum of 5 wines (applicable to purchase).

TOURS: Available on request. Tours during October harvest include crush and winemaking.

THE WINES: Cabernet Sauvignon, Chardonnay, Late Harvest Zinfandel, Merlot, Pinot Noir, Symphony (Muscat, Grenache Gris), Zinfandel.

SPECIALTIES: Pinot Noir, Chardonnay, Zinfandel.

WINEMAKERS: Tom Rodrigues; Kerry Damskey, consulting winemaker.

ANNUAL PRODUCTION: 3,000 cases.

OF SPECIAL NOTE: Tasting room/art gallery features work of owner/winemaker Tom Rodrigues. Picnic area. Winery is pet friendly. Locally made cheeses available for purchase. Occasional food-and-wine pairings offered. Events include Crab & Wine Days (January), Barrel Tasting (July), Yorkville Highlands Wine Festival (August), Mendocino Wine Affair (September), and Mushroom and Wine Days (November). Most wines sold only in the tasting room.

NEARBY ATTRACTION: Hendy Woods State Park (redwood groves, hiking, camping).

The Yorkville Highlands appellation is a scenic, sparsely populated region along Highway 128, between Anderson Valley to the northwest and Alexander Valley to the southeast. Maple Creek Winery is a hidden treasure in this relaxed, country setting—a secluded retreat where visitors can sample Pinot Noir, Chardonnay, Zinfandel, and other wines that consistently win top awards in international competitions. A narrow road leads from Highway 128 nearly a mile uphill to a rustic farm building turned tasting room. Picnic tables, Adirondack chairs, and a 1920s flatbed truck sit in the yard amid oak, maple, and fir trees. Indoors, a sign above the entrance to the barrel room summarizes the Maple Creek tasting room experience: "Enter as strangers, leave as friends."

The potential for this type of intimate experience was one of the main reasons Tom Rodrigues decided to open his own winery. Rodrigues had established himself as a successful artist in media ranging from stained glass to wine labels, such as those for Far Niente, Dolce, and Nickel & Nickel in Napa Valley, and was also known for his fine art oil painting. He also had a longtime passion for wine. His Portuguese grandparents earned their living growing fruit, and wine was regarded as merely one more food product on the family's dining room table. By the 1990s, Rodrigues had become a serious wine consumer and collector, and dreamt of living in the country with horses, cats, and dogs, growing grapes, making wine, and enjoying the fruits of his labor.

In 2001 Rodrigues purchased a 180-acre ranch in Yorkville, which includes seven natural springs, pastureland, and forests, and supports an array of wildlife. Maple Creek, the winery namesake, runs year-round through the hilly property. Today, Rodrigues farms ten acres of sustainable vineyards that produce fruit for the winery's estate Merlot and Chardonnay. He also purchases grapes from local growers who use either sustainable or organic farming methods. Rodrigues handcrafts his wine with, as he says, "passionate artistry and attention to detail," elements that are part of his creative nature, with guidance from renowned consulting winemaker Kerry Damskey.

Rodrigues decorated the tasting room with many of his works, ranging from a portrait of baseball player Cool Papa Bell (the original hangs in the Hall of Fame in Cooperstown, New York) to pastoral scenes of Anderson Valley, which adorn the winery's Artevino label. The name represents Rodrigues's twin interests in art and wine. He and his winery dogs, Buster and Posey, are often on hand to greet visitors—all part of the friendly, laidback experience Rodrigues has offered since the winery's beginnings.

Exhibit
"AROMA"

PHILLIPS HILL WINERY

A drive along scenic Highway 128 from the Mendocino Coast or the inland Redwood Highway leads to picturesque Anderson Valley. Vineyards blanket many of the creekside meadows and mountain slopes. Hints of the region's history dot the landscape: sheep graze on verdant hillsides, and apple orchards edge many a vineyard. Tall, vented cupolas—the hallmark of the valley's historic apple-dryer barns—rise from the rooftops.

One beautifully preserved example of these cupolas sits atop the Phillips Hill Winery tasting room, housed in a restored, two-story apple-dryer barn from the 1880s. The site retains many elements from its past: weathered redwood siding milled from trees grown on the property, apple-drying equipment, and a tin-roofed antique fruit stand. It occupies a peaceful corner of the eight-hundred-acre Valley Foothill Vineyards, amid apple, pear, and willow trees; ponds; and grapevines. On fair-weather days, visitors gather on a deck over a bubbling creek to taste wine-maker Toby Hill's latest creations.

Hill's career as a winemaker came about as a natural turn in an ever-evolving journey. Having earned a bachelor's degree in fine arts from the California College of the Arts, he worked as an artist in New York in the 1980s, then in 1989 moved back to San Francisco, where he was born. Hill launched an architectural colorist business but yearned to live in a more rural area, where he could design and build a barn-style residence with ample space for his pursuits. In 1997 he purchased thirty acres on Greenwood Ridge and completed construction on his home in a summer.

Hill became enamored with the excellent quality of Mendocino's Pinot Noir wines. In 2002 he heard that a local winemaker had four barrels of Oppenlander Vineyard Pinot Noir for sale and jumped at the opportunity to purchase the wine to create something in a new medium. He founded Phillips Hill Winery (Phillips is a family name) and began producing his own wine. Apart from mentoring with local winemakers for his first vintage, Hill largely taught himself the craft and discovered that he had a natural affinity for winemaking. Today Hill continues to focus on Pinot Noir and also makes small lots of Chardonnay and Gewürztraminer. He sources fruit from Valley Foothill Vineyards and other established growers in the Anderson Valley AVA, as well as Mendocino Ridge and Comptche in the Mendocino AVA. Hill runs the winery with fiancée Natacha Durandet, a native of the Loire Valley in France. Durandet, who has extensive culinary experience, occasionally prepares and serves French-inspired foods to complement wines sampled on the barn's second floor, which has framed illustrations of Phillips Hill Winery labels, each designed by Toby Hill.

PHILLIPS HILL WINERY
5101 Hwy. 128
Philo, CA 95466
707-895-2209
wine@phillipshill.com
phillipshill.com

OWNER: Toby Hill.

LOCATION: 4 miles northwest of Philo.

APPELLATIONS: Anderson Valley, Mendocino Ridge, Mendocino.

HOURS: 10:30 A.M.–5 P.M. daily.

TASTINGS: $5 (waived with purchase). Reservations required for groups of 8 or more.

TOURS: By appointment.

THE WINES: Chardonnay, Gewürztraminer, Pinot Noir, Tempranillo.

SPECIALTY: Pinot Noir.

WINEMAKER: Toby Hill.

ANNUAL PRODUCTION: 1,800 cases.

OF SPECIAL NOTE: Winery is pet friendly. Tastings held in 130-year-old apple-dryer barn. Artisan cheeses and charcuterie plates available upon request. Most wines available only in tasting room.

NEARBY ATTRACTIONS: Hendy Woods State Park (hiking, camping); Navarro River (swimming, fishing, wildlife viewing).

RIVINO ESTATE WINERY

RIVINO ESTATE WINERY
4001 Cox-Schrader Rd.
Ukiah, CA 95482
707-293-4262
Jason@rivino.com
rivino.com

OWNERS: Jason McConnell and Suzanne Jahnke-McConnell.

LOCATION: 2 miles south of Ukiah via Cox-Schrader Rd. exit off U.S. 101.

APPELLATION: Mendocino.

HOURS: 10 A.M.–5 P.M. daily.

TASTINGS: $8 for 5 wines.

TOURS: Estate tour and tasting ($75), including vineyard tour by 2-seat Kubota vehicle and cheese pairing alongside Russian River, by appointment.

THE WINES: Cabernet Franc, Chardonnay, Coferment (Syrah, Viognier), Pinot Blanc, Rosé of Cabernet Franc, Rosé of Syrah; Sangiovese, Sedulous (Bordeaux blend), Viognier.

SPECIALTIES: Limited-production, single-vineyard estate wines.

WINEMAKER: Jason McConnell.

ANNUAL PRODUCTION: 3,500 cases.

OF SPECIAL NOTE: Picnic tables on deck and surrounding grounds overlooking vineyards. Winery is pet friendly. Live music, wine, and food every Friday night, weather permitting. Annual events include the Wine & Swine roast and barbecue (June/July). All fruit is estate grown. Most wines available only in the tasting room.

NEARBY ATTRACTIONS: Lake Mendocino (hiking, boating, fishing, camping); Grace Hudson Museum (Pomo Indian baskets, historical photographs).

At the southern edge of Ukiah, the Russian River flows through a pastoral valley on its journey southwest toward Sonoma County and the Pacific Ocean. The 212-acre Schrader Ranch—home of Rivino Estate Winery—edges the western banks of the river. The name (combining *river* and *vino*) pays homage to the mighty waterway, visible from nearly every vantage point at the winery's hilltop perch, and the wines, all made on-site from carefully tended estate grapes. Visitors to Rivino's rustic tasting room are treated to panoramic picture-perfect views of the river valley and an expanse of vineyards stretching east toward oak-studded hills.

Canadian law professor Gordon Jahnke purchased the Schrader Ranch in 1993. He had visited Mendocino County while on sabbatical at U.C. Berkeley and was enamored by the beauty of the Ukiah Valley. A native Saskatchewan farm boy who also appreciated fine wines, Jahnke vowed to move one day to Mendocino and enter the grape-growing business. Twenty years later, his dream became reality. At the time he purchased the ranch, it was planted mostly with pear trees. Over the next several years, the property was replanted with grapevines. Today Schrader Ranch Vineyard produces Chardonnay, Cabernet Franc, Viognier, Pinot Blanc, Merlot, and Sangiovese.

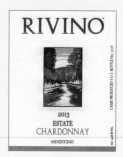

For more than a decade, the vineyard sold nearly all its grapes to other winemakers. Gordon Jahnke's daughter, Suzanne, had moved to the ranch in the mid-1990s and met her future husband, Jason McConnell, at a Mendocino County wine-tasting event. They built a home on the ranch and began to make small amounts of wine for themselves. Their hobby became a passion, and they founded Rivino Estate Winery in 2008. They continue to sell 95 percent of their grapes to others, including local winemakers such as Navarro Vineyards and Handley Cellars. However, they reserve the vineyard's best lots to handcraft limited quantities of wines, including a highly acclaimed Viognier and Sedulous, a Bordeaux blend largely of Merlot and Cabernet Franc. Each bottle displays the number of cases produced and the bottle's individual identification number. The Rivino labels, designed by Canadian artist Cameron Bird, depict the seductive Russian River scene.

McConnell, an engineer with construction management experience, added a deck and fire pit next to the winery. He also built the cinderblock tasting room, whose wall enclosures open to the deck, and planted jasmine, chocolate cosmos, thyme, and other plants that reflect wine aromas. Redwood, valley oak, and bay trees surround the tasting room grounds, where locals gather every Friday evening to feast on Rivino wines, listen to live music, and take in the views of the river and valley.

ACKNOWLEDGMENTS

Creativity, perseverance, integrity, and commitment are fundamental qualities for guaranteeing the success of a project. The artistic and editorial teams who worked on this edition possess these qualities in large measures. My heartfelt thanks go to K. Reka Badger, Cheryl Crabtree, Daniel Mangin, and Marty Olmstead, writers; Robert Holmes, photographer; Judith Dunham, copyeditor; Linda Bouchard, proofreader; Poulson Gluck Design, production; Scott Runcorn, color correction; Ben Pease, cartographer; and Linda Siemer, administration.

In addition, I am grateful for the invaluable counsel and encouragement of Chester and Frances Arnold; Greg Taylor; Beth Costa and Anne Loupy of The Wine Road, Northern Sonoma County; my esteemed parents — Estelle Silberkleit and William Silberkleit; Danny Biederman; and the scores of readers and winery enthusiasts who have contacted me over the past decade to say how much they enjoy this book series.

I also extend my deepest appreciation to Ann Everett-Cotroneo and the staff of the Hampton Inn in the town of Ukiah, California, and Herman Seidell of MacCallum House in the town of Mendocino, California, as well as Liat Pardini and the staff of the Geyserville Inn of Geyserville, California, for their excellent hospitality and enthusiastic support of this project.

And finally, for her love and creative input, as well as for enduring work-filled weekends and midnight deadlines, my gratitude and affection go to Lisa Silberkleit.

— Tom Silberkleit

OTHER BOOKS BY WINE HOUSE PRESS

The California Directory of Fine Wineries — Central Coast
Santa Barbara • San Luis Obispo • Paso Robles

Also available in e-book format for iPad, Kindle, Kobo, Nook, and other tablets.

Wine House Press
127 East Napa Street, Suite E, Sonoma, CA 95476
707-996-1741

Editor and publisher: Tom Silberkleit
Original design: Jennifer Barry Design
Production: Poulson Gluck Design
Copyeditor: Judith Dunham
Cartographer: Ben Pease
Color correction: Eviltron
Artistic development: Lisa Silberkleit
Proofreader: Linda Bouchard

All photographs by Robert Holmes, except the following:
page 40, bottom left: Ehlers Estate; page 49: Lisa Sze; page 55, bottom left: T. Nycek Photography; page 78: courtesy Sterling Vineyards; page 101, bottom left: Dennis De La Montanya; page 102, bottom right: Scott Chebegria; page 104 and page 105, bottom left: Steven Rothfeld; page 106, bottom left, and page 107: Chad Keig; page 109, bottom left: Charlie Gesell; page 109, bottom right: courtesy Gary Farrell Vineyards and Winery; page 110, bottom left: Paige Green; page 115: George Rose; page 116: Avis Mandel; page 117, bottom left and center: Matt Armendariz; page 117, bottom right: Duncan Garrett; page 135: Peter Griffith Photography; page 150: Tom Liden.

Front cover photograph: Goldeneye, Anderson Valley, CA
Back cover photographs: top left: Domaine Carneros; top right: Beringer Vineyards;
bottom left: Swanson Vineyards; bottom right: Robert Mondavi Winery.

Printed and bound in China through Imago Sales (USA) Inc.
ISBN-13: 978-0-9853628-3-6

Seventh Edition

Distributed by Publishers Group West, 1700 Fourth Street, Berkeley, CA 94710, www.pgw.com

The publisher has made every effort to ensure the accuracy of the information contained in
The California Directory of Fine Wineries, but can accept no liability for any loss, injury, or inconvenience
sustained by any visitor as a result of any information or recommendation contained in this guide.
Travelers should always call ahead to confirm hours of operation, fees, and other highly variable information.

Always act responsibly when drinking alcoholic beverages by selecting a designated driver or prearranged transportation.

Customized Editions

Wine House Press will print custom editions of this volume for bulk purchase at your request. Personalized covers and
foil-stamped corporate logo imprints can be created in large quantities for special promotions or events, or as premiums.
For more information, contact Custom Imprints, Wine House Press, 127 E. Napa Street, Suite E, Sonoma, CA 95476; 707-996-1741.

Join the Facebook Fan Page: www.facebook.com/CaliforniaFineWineries
Follow us on Twitter: twitter.com/cafinewineries
Scan to visit our website: www.CaliforniaFineWineries.com

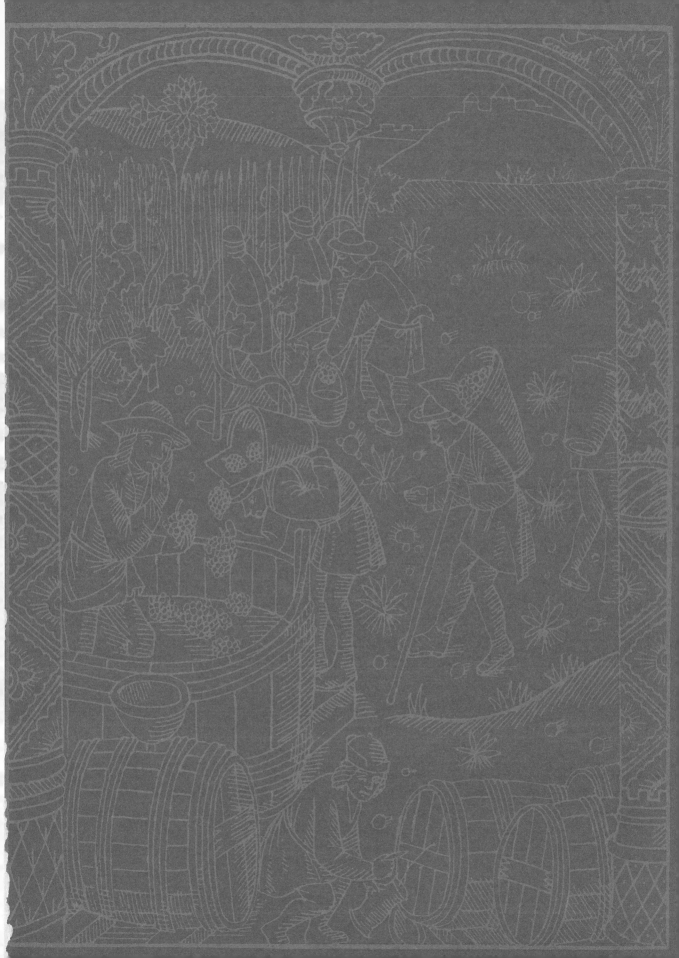